Guys Just Don't Kiss Like That

Mary Dytyniak

Second Edition

I0116068

LIFE RATTLE PRESS
TORONTO, ON
ISBN 978 - 1 - 897161 - 82 - 1
CP 789 - 1 - 78954 - 34 - 1

Published in Canada by Life Rattle Press
Life Rattle Press
247 Roxton Road
Toronto, Ontario, Canada
M6G 3R1

Library and Archives Canada Cataloguing in Publication

Dytyniak, Mary, 1988-
Guys just don't kiss like that / Mary Dytyniak.

ISBN 978-1-897161-82-1

1. Dytyniak, Mary, 1988-. 2. Coming out (Sexual orientation).
3. Lesbians--Canada--Biography. I. Title.

HQ75.4.D98A3 2010   306.76'63092   C2010-901929-6

Life Rattle new publishers series, ISSN 1713-8981

Editing by Marianne Kalich and Su Lyn Liew
Copy Edited by John Dunford
Book Design by Miriam Olszewski
Cover Illustration by Amanda Haller
Chapter Illustration by Cyrille Viola

Printed and bound in Canada

Contents

Chapter 1: A Night Out at the Barone Rosso

Evelyn looks at me from across the table, a Bellini cocktail at her lips. I smile at her. The air is balmy; the heat of the day clinging to our skin as dusk settles on the small city of Siena, Italy. The roughly hewn brick walls of shops, restaurants and cafés hug narrow streets worn by the footsteps of locals and tourists.

My friends and I from the University of Toronto Summer Abroad program sit outside a two-storey restaurant just off of Via Banchi di Sotto Street. We sip ice-cold orange juice and champagne Bellinis, a toast to our newfound friendship. We met at the beginning of the week at a student lunch of pizza, pasta and wine that encouraged mingling under the hot Tuscan sun. Our group formed naturally, none of us knowing anyone in the program. I just wanted a chance to talk to Evelyn.

"You still wanna' grab those shots guys? Soviets are two for five Euros tonight." I ask the table. Our waiter, five foot seven with short black hair, donning a white dress shirt, a black tie and a disdain-ful expression, places two rye and gingers in front of Anthony and

Amanda.

"It's not my fault I speak poor Italian." Anthony shrugs and picks up his drink.

Amanda nods and grabs hers. "I said ciao. That should count for something right?" They laugh and clink their glasses.

Amanda and Anthony are both quirky, but in different ways. Anthony is a slim first-year student studying music and composition at the St. George campus downtown. He's a bit nerdy, easy going and friendly. Being gay, he acts as our decoy at bars to fend off aggressive Italian men inching in on us as we drink and dance. Amanda just finished her second year in English, Philosophy and Film studies. I haven't quite pinned her yet. She admits to being bi-curious, cops a feel of women's breasts when drunk and is intellectual, clever and slightly mischievous with short brown hair.

"Anyways." Evelyn shakes her head at them, smiling. "I'd be down for some shots. That is if I have someone to split them with..." She glances at me.

"Oh." I blink. "I'm down."

"Cool." She smiles and continues sipping her drink. I look her up and down as she pokes her straw into the melting orange slush of her Bellini.

Is she into me?

Her damp wavy black hair with white-blonde highlights cascades down her neck and chest. Images flash through my mind of us squeezing up against one another at the bar and my inhibitions slipping away. Voices grow distant as my mind wanders. We had spent the day at Ossessione Beach, drinking cans of Heineken, tossing around a volleyball and listening to Evelyn read our Tarot cards while lying in the sand.

***

"Oh, well isn't that interesting." Evelyn read my fortune aloud. "You find yourself in unfamiliar territory and are holding back when it comes to a future romantic opportunity. Let go of your fear. Now is the time."

I chuckled nervously.

"Why won't you just tell us who you have a crush on, Mary?"

Alex asked in a tired voice, lounging in her leopard print bikini. "We won't care."

"It is a girl, right?" Evelyn peered at me.

Amanda glanced up from one of her course novels, *Death in Venice* and winked. "Yes, she did admit to that."

I blushed, but didn't answer.

"Well, whoever it is, I'm sure you won't have a problem getting them. Those two are already drooling over you." Evelyn nodded towards Matt and Mario as they threw the volleyball back and forth near the ocean surf.

I shrugged and let a smile slip.

Evelyn scoffed. "Of course you'd be cocky. The hot ones always are."

***

Alex taps my arm. "Well? Are we going to the bar or what? I'm bored, let's go dancing."

"Yeah, yeah, okay." I nod. "But I need to be drunk for that."

"That can be arranged." Alex grins and runs her fingers through her long, straight brown hair. Her green eyes fill with mirth. I can't help but laugh at her enthusiasm. Alex is another first-year, eager to party and meet guys. We hit it off immediately, spending our afternoons together at cafés, sipping espresso and exchanging stories with Katherine. Katherine and I met earlier, at our summer job working the graduation ceremonies at U of T. She was quieter than me at first, but I soon warmed up to her sarcasm and self-deprecating humour. We're both entering our fourth year in September.

"I'm not touching any alcohol after my little display last time." Katherine laughs. "But I'll watch. You guys can be my entertainment."

Katherine drank a bottle-and-a-half of Chianti wine at the Contrada dinner organized to welcome U of T students to the five-week program. She threw up her salad, pasta and pork sausage over the stone balcony and onto the local monk's football field. I held back the tiny blonde curls of her hair as the vomit streamed out. She calls her hair 'The Jew Fro'.

I polish off my Bellini and look directly at Evelyn. "Okay, let's get this shit started."

***

The Barone Rosso placard hangs above open wooden doors covered in peeling green paint. Lanterns cemented into brick-façade walls light up Via del Rialto Street. Cigarette smoke wafts through the balmy air. It's 11 p.m. The nearby pizzeria, café and laundromat are closed. Immigrant Serbians and local Italians loiter on the street corner. They watch us as Anthony leads our group up the narrow street and into the bar.

The Barone Rosso is poorly lit and reeks of stale beer. Men in their mid to late twenties grope us with their eyes. We stride past them and wait at the bar. "I Gotta Feeling" by the Black Eyed Peas pounds from speakers on the empty dance floor. Students from our program hover nearby. Locals sit on wooden chairs and talk across round tables.

"I got a feelin'/ That tonight's gonna be a good night / That tonight's gonna be a good night / That tonight's gonna be a good, good night"

A bartender with bristly black facial hair leans over fresh glasses, the sink and liquor bottles. "Ciao. What can I get you?"

"Due soviet shots per favore," Evelyn shouts across the bar.

I point to the tap. "A pint of Heineken."

The bartender nods, lines up two shot glasses and pours white-spiced rum. He hands Evelyn a plate filled with sugar, ground espresso and lemon wedges. He fills a tall, clear glass with Heineken draft.

"Dieci."

I pull a pink ten Euro bill from my black pocket and hand it to him. "Grazie." He nods and moves on to the next customer.

Evelyn turns to face me. "So, you said you're from Mississauga, right?"

"Yup." I place a shot in front of her and pull mine closer.

"I grew up in Richmond Hill. Not much to do in the burbs' beside drink eh?" Her lips curl into a smile.

I chuckle and nod. "Yeah, pretty much."

We rub our lemon wedges into the sugar and espresso and pick up our shot glasses. "Well, cheers." I hold my shot up to hers.

She moves closer, reminding me of just how short she is. She smiles coyly and clinks her shot glass against mine. "Cheers, Mary."

We throw back the Soviets. Evelyn winces and bites into the lemon wedge. I chug my beer.

"You're definitely from the burbs." Evelyn smirks.

I run my eyes over her small frame, the alcohol washing over me. "Shall we?"

I follow Evelyn to the dance floor. We find our friends as they laugh and jump up and down to the music. They open their circle for us. Evelyn and I slide in. American Top 40 songs reverberate through the bar. I down my glass of Heineken and place it on an empty table. Evelyn sways to the music. Her purple T-shirt fits loosely around her shoulders and clings to her breasts. She wears tight black shorts and gladiator sandals that hug her ankles. We stare at each other and grin. I take a step forward.

Should I dance with her? God, she looks hot.

I turn to Anthony and pump my arms to the rhythm of the music. Anthony's face flushes as he laughs, shaking his arms over his head.

"Mary," a voice yells. I turn around. Mario grabs my shoulder. His black dress shirt is unbuttoned at the neck, the warm strobe lights dance on his dark Peruvian skin.

"Hey Mario! Where'd you come from?"

"I heard a bunch of people were coming here tonight. I was looking all over for you. Why didn't you tell me you were leaving?"

Evelyn watches us.

Mario follows me around like a puppy. He bought me lunch today, stared at me in my bikini and hasn't stopped smiling since we met. "Sorry, I didn't know you were coming out tonight."

"Yeah, no problem."

Mario enters the circle and starts to dance in front of me. I glance at Evelyn. She dances with Amanda. I slide my arm around Mario's neck and grind against him. "Woo hoo!" Mario shouts and grabs my waist.

We try to move to the beat of the music, but his body feels too close to mine. Beads of sweat glisten on his neck. I catch a whiff of the overpowering scent of his Old Spice deodorant and wince. I spin around and pull away. I stumble over to Alex.

"I need some air. Wanna' go outside?" I yell into her ear.

"Yeah, sure!" she shouts.

Evelyn overhears us. "I'll come out too."

"Oh." Katherine waves. "I'm coming. I want a cigarette."

The street outside is packed with men. We cross the cobblestone street, sit down on a door-stoop and stretch our legs. Katherine pulls out a pack of red Marlboros and a lighter. We each grab a cigarette and light up.

"Man, it's fucking hot in there." Alex stands up and paces in front of us.

"Yeah, no shit eh?" Evelyn ashes her cigarette into an empty beer can. "There's too many people in there."

Alex eyes a group of Serbian men a few feet down the street. "There are some hot guys here tonight though."

Evelyn laughs. "Uh, no thanks. They're all yours, Alex."

I smile.

"More for us, right?" Alex nudges my arm.

I eye the Serbians. "Uh, nah man. They're not really floating my boat."

There are definitely some good looking guys in town, but as soon as I spotted Evelyn my gaze shifted. She made no effort to grab my attention. Subtle indications of her attraction to me were all I had to go on. I came down the stairs in Matteoli Residence the other day in a short, black skirt and a fitted T-shirt. She grinned and stared but continued chatting with Amanda. I never had to chase guys. The mystery Evelyn exuded made her sexy as hell.

"So, are you more into girls or guys right now, Mary?" Evelyn asks.

"Oh, um…" I hesitate. "Girls, I'd say."

"Sa-weet." Evelyn smiles. "Point one for our team."

I blush and inhale on my cigarette. I can feel Evelyn's eyes on me.

"Do you mind me asking if you've ever slept with a girl?"

"No." I shake my head. "It's fine. I haven't. Just made out… at clubs and stuff."

"I've made out with girls for fun too." Alex interrupts.

Evelyn nods, soaking up the information. "Ah, I see..."

Her thigh brushes against mine. I stare at my leg as it freezes into place.

"And how was the sex with guys?" Evelyn takes a drag of her cigarette and holds it between her fingers.

"I haven't had sex with a guy. Everything but."

Evelyn turns to face me, her eyes wide. "You're a virgin?!"

I chuckle. My palms start to sweat. "Yup." I lean over Evelyn and sprinkle ash into the beer can. Her natural scent holds me there for a second. I lean back.

"Wow." Evelyn blinks. "If that's not a red flag then I don't know what is. A 21-year-old virgin. You're totally a lesbian."

I stare at Evelyn. "I'm twenty actually. And I'm still figuring it out."

Katherine hovers in front of us, smoking and listening. She tries to hide a smile.

Evelyn squishes her cigarette butt into the brick wall and lets it fall into the beer can. "Yeah, take your time, but I'm pretty sure you're gay."

"Well, I don't know about that..."

"My advice to you." Evelyn continues. "When you're having sex with a girl, pay attention to her breathing and just let it flow. It'll feel really natural." Evelyn leans against me. "Aww yay! Another one for the lezzie team."

I force a smile, not knowing if that statement makes me her comrade or a potential lover. Alex stares at me with raised eyebrows. I glance past Evelyn at Katherine. She nudges her head towards Evelyn. Repeatedly.

I glare. "We should head back inside."

Katherine rolls her eyes and laughs. "Yes, I want to show you guys my sexy dance moves." She shakes her head and twirls her arms. "See, see? More of this to come!"

"Let's do it." Evelyn stands up. She offers me her hand and hoists me up. "Wow, you're really light, Mary."

"Yeah." I laugh. "I'm all skin and bones."

Evelyn looks me up and down. "I'd hardly say that." She grins, she turns and she trails behind Katherine and Alex.

Holy shit.

I watch Evelyn's pale thighs rub against each other as she crosses the cobblestone street. A wave of music spills through the open doors and Evelyn disappears inside. I bite my lower lip, scan the street and press my hand against the peeling paint of the Barone Rosso's doors.

Tonight really is going to be a good night.

Chapter 2: Courtyard Hash

Students had been craving marijuana since we arrived in Siena. But no one knew how strict the local drug laws were and if Italians even smoked weed. Opportunities often crop up in the strangest of places. In Connor's case, he walked right into one. Connor asked one of the residence staff for a cigarette on his way out of Matteoli Residence. The cigarette he toked had more than tobacco packed inside. I ditched the Il Cambio nightclub with Anthony, Evelyn and Alex, and jetted back to residence as soon as I heard the good news.

***

Francesco, the attendant at Matteoli's porter desk tonight, looks up from the 13-inch TV stowed underneath the desk. Two public telephones hang on the wall beside the laundry room, vending machines stand near the entrance, and at the end of the foyer, a wide stone staircase twists and turns four times before reaching the second floor.

A heavyset stranger sits on one of the soft blue couches next to the vending machines. His curly, short brown hair sticks to his sweating face covered in scruffy facial hair. He wears beige khakis and an A.C. Siena soccer jersey that resembles an NHL referee jersey, just as Connor had described. He laughs at a video; the volume bursting from the laptop speakers. An open bag of potato chips and two empty Peroni beer bottles lay scattered on the table in front of him.

I nudge Anthony. "What should we say?" I whisper.

"I don't know." Anthony laughs. "Favore alcuni hashish?"

I giggle.

"Yeah, man," Evelyn says. "Why not?"

"Let me do it guys." Alex cuts in. "Your Italian is terrible. He won't know what you're talking about."

Alex is fluent in Serbian, French, English, and German, and is pretty damn close to mastering Italian. I've been relying on her to help me order food, ask for directions and buy train tickets.

Alex marches up to him. "Buona sera, signore."

The man's bloodshot eyes drift towards Alex. "Ciao." He nods. "Buona sera."

"Ciao. Sono Alex." Alex places her hand on her chest.

"Buona sera. Mi chiamo Vincenzo." He wipes his large, greasy hand on his jeans and extends it to Alex.

"Noi vogliamo comprare un po di hash." Alex rubs her fingers together.

"Tutti voi?" Vincenzo looks at us.

"Sì." Alex nods.

"What is she saying?" I whisper to Evelyn. She shrugs. "No idea."

"Ti posso dare due sigaretta, va bene?" Vincenzo asks. "Sì. Grazie, grazie."

Anthony squeezes my arm. "Oh, grat-zee. I heard her say grat-zee. She must have got it. Yay!" Anthony raises his palm for a high five.

I squeal and clap his hand. "Thank god for Alex. We're getting hash!"

Vincenzo smiles at us, waves and walks out into the courtyard behind Matteoli. Alex strolls up to us, stops and waits until Vincenzo is out of earshot. "Okay, so his name is Vincenzo. He offered to smoke us for free. Just let me do the talking, okay?"

The three of us nod and follow Alex into the empty courtyard. The night air is warm and dry compared to the broiling daytime temperatures. Summers in Siena can reach up to 45 degrees. Tall, dark trees with thick branches and full leaves canopy the stone benches, gravel floor and low stone walls enclosing the area. With all the students out at Il Cambio, it's unusually quiet.

Vincenzo sits at a stone table, lights a Marlboro cigarette and opens a bottle of Peroni. He motions for us to sit down.

"Grazie." Evelyn smiles and sits beside him. I slide onto the cool stone bench beside Anthony.

Vincenzo pulls out two cigarettes and splits them vertically with a key. He reaches into his pocket and pulls out a small, brown chunk of hashish wrapped in newspaper. He pinches the hash wad and holds it up for us. "Good, yes?"

Evelyn's eyes widen. "Sì, sì."

Evelyn's been experimenting with drugs since high school. She's popped ecstasy, chewed 'shrooms, smoked weed and hash, snorted cocaine and ingested ketamine. Evelyn wants to give up pot when she returns to Toronto. It's the last of her experiments.

"Haha, sì!" Vincenzo nods and turns to Evelyn. "You speak Italiano?"

"Uh, no, no." Evelyn shakes her head. "Very little." Evelyn holds the tips of her fingers together. "Un poco."

"Ah, sì." Vincenzo laughs. "Molto bene."

"Haha, grazie."

Vincenzo holds the flame of his lighter over the hash.

"What's he doing?" I ask Evelyn.

"He's softening the hash. It's a little brick. You can't roll it like that."

Vincenzo looks at me and taps Alex's arm. "Cosa stanno dicendo?"

Alex nods. "She's explaining what you're doing." She points to Evelyn. "Uh, loro... spiegano cosa. Hm. Tu fai."

"Ah." He smiles at me. "Sì."

Vincenzo places the wad between his palms and rubs back and

forth until the hash crumbles. He opens his palms and dribbles the hash into the open cigarettes. He rolls them tightly, licks them and re-seals them.

"Cool," I whisper.

Anthony nods. "Yeah, I've never seen someone roll hash before."

"Me neither."

Vincenzo lights the hash cigarette and inhales until it catches. He holds it up to Evelyn. "Signora?"

"Si, grazie." Evelyn pinches the cigarette, tokes three times and passes it to me.

I toast to Vincenzo with the cigarette in hand. "Mucho grazie." I take a long drag. Alex cracks up laughing. "What?" I cough. "I said thank you."

The light from the lamppost shines on Alex's smirking face. "You're so funny. You just said 'much thank you'. And mucho is Spanish, not Italian."

Evelyn and Anthony chuckle.

"Oh." I blush. "My bad. Well, whatever. I tried." I inhale twice and pass the cigarette to Anthony. A rush hits my head. "Whoa." I smile, my skin tingling. "That didn't take long."

"Take it easy there, Mary." Evelyn cocks her eyebrow. "It's not a normal joint. There's tobacco mixed in."

My smile stretches into a grin. "Okay, Evelyn."

The cigarette burns out after making two full rounds to each of us.

Zykima and Amanda's voices echo in the foyer. Their sandals clack on the linoleum floor as they approach the entrance to the courtyard. They spot us and wave wildly. "Hey guys!" Zykima shouts. "I think I'm really drunk!" Her eyes bulge. She throws her purse onto the table. She and Amanda squish in beside us, their cheeks flushed.

"Jesus," Alex mutters. "What were you guys drinking?"

"I introduced Zykima to those Soviet shots." Amanda throws her arm around Zykima and wiggles her eyebrows. "She likes."

Zykima is a shy first year in Amanda and Evelyn's English class. She's a momma's girl and has never touched drugs or alcohol until this trip. Naturally, we've taken it upon ourselves to corrupt her.

"Zykima," Evelyn hisses. "Chill out. There are people sleeping upstairs."

Zykima giggles. "Okay," she whispers. "Gotcha." She taps her nose and winks.

"How was Il Cambio?" I ask.

"I feel good," Amanda says in her deep, Barry White voice. "Do you feel gooood?" Amanda leers at me.

The tingling sensation has spread to my entire body. "I feel amazing." I press my fingers into my cheeks and giggle. "I feel like putty."

Amanda bobs her head up and down, grinning. "Niiice."

Vincenzo's cell phone lights up, vibrates and beeps. "Ugh, scusa."

"Sooo, Mary," Amanda slurs as she leans her elbows on the table and leers at me. "We think we've figured out who you like."

Zykima nods excitedly.

"Oh, yeah?" I laugh.

I catch Evelyn smiling out of the corner of my eye.

"We think it rhymes with…" Amanda whispers into my ear. Her hot breath tickles my earlobe. "Mevelyn."

I roll my eyes, unable to hide my smirk. "I told you! I'm not telling you."

"It totally is!" Amanda wags her finger in my face. "I knew it!" I shake my head, blushing.

Vincenzo shouts into his phone a few feet away, kicking at the stone gravel.

Evelyn peers at me, her eyes narrowing. "I think I might know who it is too… that or I have absolutely no clue."

We lock eyes. I grip the stone bench. Warm air brushes against my body as I stare at her, paralyzed.

She knows it's her.

Vincenzo plunks down beside Evelyn, shattering our gaze.

I catch my breath.

"Uh, sorry for that. My Madre, she call me. To uh, how do you say?" Vincenzo hits his crotch with his hands. "Bust my balls. Yes, that is it."

I laugh. "That's jokes."

"That's sure as hell universal," Evelyn says. "Parents are parents no matter where you live." Evelyn smacks her hand against her palm. "Your mom?"

Vincenzo nods and laughs. "Sì! Sì!"

Our laughter echoes through the courtyard as Vincenzo pulls out another chunk of hash. I float to my room that night on a cloud of hashish, liquor and beer. I am rudely awakened by a blaring alarm clock.

Chapter 3: Espresso and Gossip

I sprawl on my single bed with the sheets hanging off the edge. A thin layer of sweat coats my skin; something I'm still getting used to despite cold afternoon showers. I lie back down on the pillow, stretch my arms above my head and close my eyes.

She was smiling at me, looking right at me. I swear she was.

I heard Evelyn with Amanda and Zykima this morning, giggling and talking loudly in the street on my way to a small grocery store just up the road. I froze when I heard her voice; a feeling I couldn't shake, a feeling that I was slowly becoming addicted to.

"Oh, look. It's Mary." Amanda called out and waved as the street sloped, bringing them closer to me. Zykima waved too, but I wasn't paying attention to them.

Evelyn held a case of water, hugging it to her chest. It slipped when she saw me, stopping just short of her hips.

Her grip tightened. "Oh. Hey Mary."

"Hi…"

And then she smiled.

I turn onto my side and glance out the window. And then she smiled...

I sigh, grinning like an idiot. I recall her voice and her lips and her eyes. I think of all the scenarios, of all the ways that I could let her know. A knock strikes the thick wooden door of my room.

I jump.

"Mary?" a familiar voice calls.

Room calls have replaced cell phones around the residence. Only a few of us have the money to pay for international phone service or to buy a cheap phone in town. A second knock strikes the wood.

I hop off the bed and swing the door open. "Hey, Alex." I smile and open the door wider.

"You bum, were you napping again?" Alex strolls into my room. She rifles through the pile of junk scattered on my desk—an open bag of chips, my laptop, my room key, my blow dryer and a 2-litre bottle of water. I've been going through two bottles a day in this heat.

I laugh and close the bag of chips. "Haha, maybe."

Alex shakes her head, cracking a smile. "Me and Katherine are grabbing coffee. You coming?"

My roommate Kirsten and her new best friend Adriana might be back soon. They've taken to huddling around her laptop to watch episodes of The Tudors whenever I'm not napping. I tried grabbing lunch with them earlier in the trip, but their conversations about professors and historical TV series and proper Italian pronunciation sent me running.

"Yeah, man. I could use an espresso."

Katherine waits for us in the student lounge, chatting with Evelyn and Amanda on the cool tile floor. I bite my lip. Evelyn wears a short gray tweed skirt and a red halter-top. She looks up from her laptop and smiles at us. "Hey there."

"Hey guys," my voice squeaks. I clear my throat and glance at the laptop. "Checking Facebook?"

"Yeah, just responding to Sonya's messages."

"Oh." My expression falls flat. I fiddle with the room key tucked into my jean shorts pocket. Evelyn's face is glued to the screen.

Tap tap. Tap. Tap tap tap.

Ugh. Whatever.

"Are you ready to go, Katherine?"

Katherine rolls her eyes. "Yes, I was waiting for you remember?"

Evelyn smirks. "You really do take your time, Mary."

"Yeah, yeah." I mutter. "Let's go."

The three of us make our way through the hilly, winding town, more confident of our path than in the first week spent veering this way and that. Katherine insists on wearing long-sleeved shirts and wrapping scarves around her neck even though it's boiling outside. She is over six feet tall with a wide build—something she is very self-conscious of. Alex walks on my other side, lean and tall with long, silky hair. She is confident in her strides, donning a loose-fitting leopard print dress, gladiator sandals, thick-framed glasses and a purple leather messenger bag.

Students from the residence smile at us as we walk past them. Locals on Vespas honk and steer around us, and the general hum of voices and movement fills the streets. Restaurants, cafés, bakeries, tobacco shops and boutiques are crammed beside one another, occupying worn, crumbling buildings that are hundreds of years old. Wooden shutters painted dark greens, soft reds and deep blues are kept wide open to welcome the warm breeze. The sun beams down on us as we enter Delcino Café.

Italian pop music plays quietly, blending with the voices of patrons. Tables and chairs line the wall and a glass display built into the espresso bar tempts us with decadent pastries covered in chocolate and filled with custard, cheese and fruit. A tanned woman in her early thirties with reddish brown hair tied into a bun stands behind the bar. She smiles and nods. "Ciao. Buona Sera." Her voice is light and feminine.

"Ciao." I nod. "Uno makiato." I roll my tongue lightly. I know few Italian words, but I try to pronounce them as best as I can. The locals are friendly and polite for the most part, so long as we try to speak their language.

The woman pauses for a moment. "Scusa?"

I speak more slowly. "Café maki-ato."

17

"Ah, café macchiato." the words roll beautifully off her tongue.
"Sì." I nod.

She smiles and nods back. "Sì."

I take a seat at the front of the café and wait for Katherine and Alex to order. I push my sunglasses onto my head and tuck my bangs behind my ears. A local newspaper lies on the table. I flip through it, scanning the headlines and photographs before closing it.

As if I read Italian.

Alex slides in beside me and hands me a small brown espresso cup topped with milk foam.

"Oh. Thanks, Alex. You didn't have to bring it over."

Alex reaches over my arm and grabs a sugar packet. "No worries."

I sip on the dark, creamy espresso topped with a thin layer of milk foam. Little cups filled with this delectable liquid are something I look forward to at least twice a day now. Alex introduced me to the café macchiato; bitter to the tongue but rich and decadent. It is the perfect excuse for a cigarette, socializing and a break from Matteoli.

Katherine drums her fingers on the table. She chuckles nervously. "So, I have something to tell you guys…"

I look at her suspiciously. "Uh huh?"

"Remember how I was telling you guys I liked someone in Mary's class?"

"Yeah." Alex nods.

I pull a mental list of all the guys in my class, mostly jocks. "Hmm. Give us a hint."

"Well, his hair colour kind of gives it away…" Katherine fiddles with the small silver spoon resting on her saucer.

"Hmm. Well, it can't be John or Leo. You already told me it wasn't them." Alex takes a sip of her drink. "Wait a minute." Her mouth drops. "Oh my god, is it Connor?!"

Katherine makes a strangling noise. "Uh, no?" She plays with her curly blonde hair.

"Connor?" I ask.

Katherine's blushes deeply, her cheeks turning red.

"Oh my god! It is Connor!" Alex blurts.

I grin. "Connor? Really?"

Katherine sighs. "He's beautiful and misunderstood."

Alex and I turn to each other with raised eyebrows and tight smiles. I try to hold it in, but Alex is about to crack. Our boisterous laughter erupts, filling the café.

Katherine glares. "Ugh, look, I know he drinks a lot, but I think he has this really sensitive side that no one else sees."

We laugh even harder. Alex snorts. A couple sitting a few tables over look up from their tiramisu dessert. They glance at us and continue their conversation in Italian. Katherine crosses her arms over her chest. "That's the last time I tell you jerks anything!"

I place my hand over my mouth to suppress my mirth. "I'm sorry, Katherine, but he's in my class and all he does is sleep 'cause he's hung-over every morning. He's nice enough, but he's just so obnoxious."

Alex puts her glasses back on, having wiped the tears from her eyes. "I'm sorry, I didn't mean to laugh."

I grin. "Me neither."

Alex sits upright and clears her throat. "Okay, so I get that Connor is pretty funny, and he is kind of cute, but really? Of all the guys here?"

"Yes, of all the guys here," Katherine says sarcastically. "Whatever, I think he's really nice."

I raise my hands in defense. "Alright, if that's what you're into. I won't judge." I pause for a moment, a grin forming on my lips. "You know, Katherine. He is in my class and sits in the back with me. I could put in a good word." I wink at her.

Katherine's eyes narrow. She slowly smiles back. "Fine, then you won't have any problem with me telling Evelyn she's the one you have a crush on."

"Don't you dare!"

The couple glares at us. "Sorry guys," I mumble.

Alex smirks and finishes her espresso. "It's not like it's a huge secret, Mary. I'm pretty sure she already knows."

I squirm in my seat. I've thought about asking Evelyn out for coffee just about every day, five times a day. Of walking up to her door one afternoon and just asking her out, but the thought of her shooting me a confused look and asking, "What for?" is just too terrifying. I've never asked a girl out before. Guys always took the lead on that front. I needed more direction.

"She might be interested, Mary," Katherine says. "She thinks you're pretty cool."

My eyes light up. "Really? What'd she say?"

Katherine laughs. "Just that you're really cute and sweet…" She pauses as if trying to recall something. "Oh, and she wonders what it would be like to kiiiiiss you." Katherine puckers her lips.

"What?!" I lean forward and slam my knee against the table, jostling my espresso.

"She did not say that, come on." Alex smacks Katherine.

"Okay, not the kissing part, but that's payback." Katherine pokes her tongue out at me.

"Ugh, you're such a jerk." I rub my knee. "That hurt."

"She called her cute though?" Alex asks.

"Yeah, she did. Honestly, I think she's interested, Mary. Besides, you might be good for her, she has a really mixed up past."

I lean forward eagerly. "You think I'd be good for her?"

Katherine nods, but her smile fades. "I don't know how much she's told you, but it doesn't sound like she's had the best relationships or has been treated very well."

"What do you mean?"

Katherine frowns. "Okay, but this stays between us."

"Yeah, of course."

"Sure."

"When she was younger, she was…" Katherine looks down into her empty cup. "Her dad's co-worker was giving her a ride home and he—"

"Oh, no," Alex mutters.

A twinge runs through me. "He what?"

Katherine's voice drops. "He put his hand on her leg and tried to…" She gestures awkwardly. "You know…" Her words trail off.

I sink into my chair. "Oh," I whisper.

Alex shakes her head. "Wow, what an asshole."

Katherine nods. "Yeah, I think it really disturbed her. She's had a lot of people try to pull that kind of stuff. It really bothers her."

"I hope she knows I would never mistreat her."

Katherine smiles. "I know you wouldn't, Mary. That's why it might be good for her if you two can connect. I know you care about her."

I absorb the information as best as I can, the conversation weighing on me. It does not change a thing though, because there is something about this girl that draws me in. And something telling me that I have to push for this.

"I really do like her," I say softly.

"I don't know if she's ready for anything long-term after the last girl." Katherine warns me. "They ended up living together when she was nineteen and the girl became really reliant on her and it just got... messy." She sighs. "It might be years before Evelyn sorts her shit out and can be there for someone else."

"Mmm, yeah. She mentioned her ex. I can do that though, even if it doesn't last as long as I would like it to. I really want to be there for her, to show her something good you know? I'm still sorting myself out too."

"Well, maybe that's what both of you need right now."

"Yeah, I just hope she's open to it."

The conversation steers away from Evelyn, but she grazes the back of my mind as we speak of more and more personal things, our friendship solidifying with each secret shed. The sun sets, enveloping the town in a golden haze of light. As we make our way back to Matteoli, the sheer romanticism and beauty of this aging place moves me closer to her.

If I don't chase this girl now, I never will.

Chapter 4: My First Kiss

I hang my damp tanks, tees and shorts on a laundry rack on the second floor of Matteoli Residence. Connor, Andrew and a few other guys chat at the end of the hallway. The wooden door of Room 38 opens and Alia steps out.

"Oh." Alia smiles at me. "Hey, Mary."

"Hey, how's it going?"

"Not too bad." She locks her door. "Just studying for the English analysis tomorrow."

"Oh." I drop a sock on the floor. "I forgot you were in that class."

Evelyn takes that class.

A bunch of us went to the Barone Rosso last night after playing cards and drinking red wine in the Piazza del Campo, a massive square in the centre of town. Evelyn and I talked over beer and Soviet shots. She stroked my lower back with her finger and grinned at me. I stopped breathing. We drifted from our friends and walked back early.

22

"So." Evelyn started, her eyes downcast as we swayed through the streets, with lampposts lighting the way back to residence. "I might have this wrong and I don't want to be arrogant, but I'm pretty sure I know who you like."

My head felt muddled from the last round. Alcohol always makes me bolder. "It is you." I shrugged. "I thought you would've guessed sooner. It's kind of obvious considering the situation."

"Well." Evelyn looked up the road. "I started thinking it might be me since I'm the only lesbian on this trip."

I chuckled as we passed the bright green medical cross glowing in front of the drug store. "Yeah, that's true."

"Wait." Evelyn stopped in the middle of the empty street. "Is it just 'cause I'm a lesbian?"

"No." I shook my head. "Not at all. You're exactly my type."

Evelyn smiled out of the corner of her lip.

We took a detour to the park overlooking the brightly lit city; just down the road from Matteoli Residence, right before the road slopes towards one of the town exits. During the day, we had gone there with our friends to sunbathe on the pale yellow grass dried by the sweltering sun and ate sweet figs hanging from low tree branches. The pathway was illuminated by the moon as we walked through the park, casting a soft glow for us to see by. We walked past the cement barrier; crumbling and marked with graffiti, to the private grass knoll hidden by an abandoned building covered in fading red brick and surrounded by a rickety wooden fence made of loosely constructed beams and posts. Trees hugged most of the fence, blocking the city, so we kept exploring until we found an opening with a spectacular view of Siena. We stared out at the town for the longest time, our eyes wandering across clay shingled houses, hilly winding streets, tall church steeples and cypress trees filling the Tuscan valley below. I had never seen anything like it. Toronto was noisy and crowded and restless. Siena was simply breathtaking.

There she was, this stunning girl with pale skin and jet-black hair, standing beside me, leaning against the wooden railing with a dreamy expression on her face. She caught my gaze and smiled, inching closer. I asked her to take off her gladiator sandals so I could see the dark ink covering her feet. She obliged, explaining that the left foot held her mother's Italian maiden name and family coat of arms and the right foot was marked with the Gaelic script of her father's family name and the Scottish crown. I ran my fingers along the ink lines, remarking that it was beautiful.

We kept the conversation going 'til 3 a.m. We talked about growing up in the suburbs with nothing better to do than drink and do drugs in our parents' basements or in nearby parks. About how our Catholic parents can't control what we do or who we sleep with. How she lost close friends after coming out to them. How scared I was to tell my family. She told me that I'd get through it, that we have to.

We lay down in the grass, sat next to one another on a bench, leaned against an old church wall and never worked up the nerve to kiss each other.

***

"Yeah, I am." Alia's voice jars me. "I still don't know what book I'm writing it on. I feel like I should be prepared with all the books though, just in case."

I pull my brown tank top out of the laundry bag slouching on the floor. "That sounds like a lot of work. Why not just pick one book and focus on that?"

"Yeah, I guess I could do that. But I dunno'."

I nod politely. "That's what I would do."

Alia twirls a long black strand of hair and gazes down the corridor. "I guess.

I scan the empty hallway. "Well anyways—"

"Hey!" she yelps. "You're going on that trip to Rome right? Are you excited?"

Jesus.

"Um, yeah I am. It should be fun. I've never been."

I avert my eyes and tersely lay out the rest of my wet clothes. It's past 10:30 p.m. I told myself I'd go visit Evelyn in her room after I finished my laundry. "Well—"

"Anyways, I guess I should go study." Alia turns to leave.

Thank god.

"Okay." I smile. "Have fun."

Alia waves and strolls away. I pick up my laundry bag and head down the hallway. I pass Zykima's room. I had knocked on her door ten minutes ago to get an update on the Evelyn situation.

***

"Mary, she's definitely interested," Zykima had said. "She said she really wanted to kiss you last night but was just waiting for the right opportunity. And then, when she walked you home, there were too many people in the hall. So, she just hugged you goodnight."

I smirked stupidly. "Really? She said that?"

Zykima's threw her hands up at me. "Just do something for god's sake. Before I do!"

"Okay, okay!" I laughed. "I'll go to her room tonight."

***

I push my door open. Bright fluorescent light from the hallway floods our dark room. My roommate Kirsten snores. I hop over my Roots backpack and a pair of scuffed flip flops, and flick the bathroom light on. I slip into a black cotton tank top with lace trimming around the cleavage and a jean skirt.

Maybe I shouldn't go. What am I going to say to her? So, about last night... hehe. Wanna' make out?

I shake my head.

Ugh.

I skip over to the bathroom and stare at my reflection in the mirror. Chestnut brown bangs sweep across my lightly tanned face and a set of golden-brown eyes return my nervous gaze. Long, straight strands of hair graze my shoulders, recently trimmed before my flight to Siena.

I take a deep breath.

Okay, you can do this. Just calm down. You've made out with tons of guys before. This is nothing.

I reach for my make-up pouch.

You don't need make-up. Just go!

I snatch my green lanyard and key and lock my door. I make a right at the common room and climb the first steps to the second floor. I freeze on the fifth step.

What the fuck am I going to say to her?

My eyes bounce off the walls, steps and ceiling.

I can't do this.

I turn around and clamber down the steps. An Asian girl sits by herself on one of the blue couch chairs a few feet away. She glances at me for a moment then continues typing on her white MacBook.

I duck into the kitchen and turn on the light. I open the fridge and stare at my peach juice and prosciutto slices.

I'm not hungry. What the fuck am I doing?

I close my eyes and slam the fridge door. The inside shelf rattles.

Stop being a pussy.

I tap the light switch off and return to the stairs. Every step, all eight, glare at me. I grab the railing and squeeze it.

One, two… Fuck it.

I dash up the stairs. Two students surf the Internet in the corner of the hallway. I cut a sharp left and walk past Room 29. Room 30. Room 31. Room 32. I stop. I stare at the dull gold metal numbers glued to the oak door.

Knock on the door.

I raise my fist. My arm trembles.

Oh my god. I'm shaking.

I pace the tiled floor. Back and forth. Back and forth. I tiptoe over to the window at the end of the hall. Clay shingled buildings of all different shapes and sizes light up Siena. Large green fields and cypress trees stretch out for miles. Vineyards filled with…

So, you came all this way to stare at a view? I shake out my arms and take a deep breath. Just do it.

I stroll back to Room 32. I hold my hand in front of the door. Knock, knock.

A bed creaks. Footsteps pad the floor. The door latch turns. Evelyn appears with a book in her hand. I look her up and down, my eyes widening. Evelyn wears a thin white undershirt, a black bra and purple lace underwear. I pull my eyes from her thighs and focus on her face.

"Hey." Evelyn smiles and grips the edge of the door.

I slouch against the wall. "Hey, how's it going?" My voice squeaks.

"Not too bad, just doing some reading." Evelyn waves the book. "What's up?

"Nothing." I shrug. "Well, I mean. I uh, just wanted to clear up things about last night." The words tumble out of my mouth. "I didn't feel like we really decided on anything."

"Okay…" She shoots me a strange look.

My pulse jumps.

A student wanders down the hallway, looks at us and continues walking. He opens his door and disappears inside.

I clear my throat. "I just wanted to make sure everything is cool. Are we cool?"

Evelyn raises her eyebrows. "Yeah." She pauses. "I'm cool. Are you cool?"

I jam my hands into my pockets to stop the trembling. "Yeah. I just wanted to make sure we're good."

Evelyn nods. Then stares. My palms sweat.

"Uh, so you're good then?" I take a step back to leave.

"Yeah. Well…" Evelyn watches me. "I definitely want to pursue something, but we only have four weeks left and… I don't want things to get awkward."

Thank god she brought it up.

"Right." I nod. "Okay." I nod again.

"And I know this must be really terrifying for you since it's new. It was for me too. So, I don't want to pressure you."

"Okay, I get that." I stand up straight. "But, I definitely don't feel pressured."

Evelyn smiles. "Okay, good."

"So." I grab the doorframe. "Should we just leave things until I get back from Rome?"

Evelyn grins. I grin back. Evelyn takes three steps towards me, shifts onto her tippy toes and presses her lips against mine. I blink. Evelyn is 5'4"; I'm 5'7". Her soft, full lips rub mine.

I close my eyes and kiss her back. My hand finds its way to her hips.

This feels so... different.

I open my eyes. Evelyn's face moves back and forth with the movement of our lips; her eyes half open. I shut my eyes and continue kissing her. I lose myself in the sensations; her wet tongue, her soft lips. I tilt my head, switch sides and enclose her lips with mine. The kiss ends.

I open my eyes, dazed.

Evelyn drops to her heels, smiling. "Well, that settles that then. I guess we'll continue things when you get back from Rome."

"Yeaaah." I smile.

"Well, have a good trip. I'll see you when you get back."

"Yeaaah." My smile broadens. I feel light-headed.

"Good night." Evelyn reaches for the door.

"Good niiight." I lean in to catch a last glimpse of Evelyn before the door shuts. I spin around and glide down the hallway.

Wow. Guys just don't kiss like that.

Chapter 5: A Creaky Mattress

Room 22 of Matteoli Residence is hot. The white stucco walls sweat and sunlight beams through the shudders of the open window. Afternoons are the hottest part of the day in Siena. But that's when my roommate Kirsten is out, so I work with what I have.

Evelyn lies on top of me. She stares at me with dark brown eyes. Her hips press against mine and the white, worn-out mattress sinks beneath our weight. Sweat soaks our skin and dampens the pillow that my head rests on. I run my stiff hand down her arm and smirk.

"Oh, so you think I'm funny, do you?" Evelyn raises her eyebrows, smiling. Black bangs with white blonde highlights frame her pale face. The rest of her hair is pulled back into a loose bun. She reminds me of a 16th century Renaissance painting; a pale, shapely young woman with dark wavy hair and soft facial features.

"No, not at all." I let out a weak laugh and shift on the mattress. The springs creak as my feet touch the black metal frame. "I'm just having a hard time trying to read you." I tuck Evelyn's bangs behind her ear.

"Me?" Evelyn jerks her head back. "Really? You're the one that's hard to read. Giving me dirty looks all the time and never returning my smiles."

My hand slides off her arm. "Aw, come on. That's not fair. I told you I was exhausted when I got back from Rome. I did smile at you in the Campo!"

I made the mistake of treating Evelyn like any other friend when I strolled into the Piazza Del Campo late Sunday night after my trip to Rome. I had no idea how to behave around a woman. If I should slide my arm around her waist or grab her hand, if I could kiss her whenever I wanted, if it was okay to whisper in her ear. To avoid seeming clingy, I kept my distance that night at the bar. Evelyn left early, pissed, but claimed she was just tired. She told everyone about the great kiss we had shared, while I acted like nothing had happened at all.

It wasn't intentional. I became self-conscious and soon, she did too. We limited our interactions to stolen glances and shy smiles over the next few days. That is, until she began to leave a trail of clues that became hard to ignore, dropping flirtatious remarks and brushing up against me in front of our friends. But, she didn't act on any of it. So, I had to take the lead. I finally asked her out for that damn cup of coffee.

Evelyn chuckles. "Mmm hmm. I guess I can let that slide. But still, you are a very composed person." She brings her lips close to mine for a brief, light kiss. Her face hovers over mine, her warm breath grazing my cheeks.

"I know, I can't help it." I kiss Evelyn's lower lip and taste wild berry lip balm. She remains still. I kiss her again. She leans back, sits on my upper thighs and grins. Dimples dot her flushed cheeks. I pull myself towards her and kiss her with tight, strong lips. She wraps her arms around my back. Our bodies tighten against one another and she pushes me onto the mattress. My eyes widen. She locks me in with her thighs.

Holy fuck.

Our lips devour each other in slow, soft measures for the next few minutes. I rub her back and squeeze her arms, not sure if I want to do anything more. Evelyn caresses my arms, back, hair and breasts. She lays kisses on my neck and chest.

Evelyn stops. She smiles.

"What?"

Evelyn tilts her head. "Are you nervous?"

"Uh," I moan. "Yeah." I nod my head up and down.

"Aw, Mary." Evelyn smiles and pecks me on the lips. "Don't be scaaared," she purrs.

I feign a smile. Evelyn kisses me again. Our lips pucker loudly. My eyes snap open. The straps of Evelyn's black tank-top with thin, multi-coloured stripes slip.

Oh my god. I can't believe I have a lesbian on top of me.

My eyes dart around the sunlit room. The green leaves hanging off the thick branches of a tall oak tree in the courtyard gleam in the sunlight. Evelyn's lips feel full and soft. Donatello and a couple of guys shout and dribble a basketball in the courtyard next door. Evelyn rubs her sweaty legs against mine.

This is your chance, just go for it.

I shut my eyes and suck on her lower lip. I can feel the tiny hole that remains from her old labret piercing. Our lips lock. Evelyn pokes the tip of her tongue into my mouth. A tingling sensation shoots through my body. I pull her in tighter and slowly drag my tongue across hers. Evelyn presses her breasts against mine. I clasp my arms around her stomach and try to guide her underneath me.

Evelyn pulls back. "Am I too heavy?"

"No." I shake my head. "Not at all. I just wanted to switch."

"Oh. Okay. No problem."

I slide to the edge of the narrow bed and give her space to lie down. Evelyn shimmies her five-foot frame up the mattress.

Creaaak.

"Wow." Evelyn laughs. "This really is a shitty bed."

"Ha! I told you. Why do you think I've been complaining?"

Evelyn shifts her weight and slips her arms around me.

Creak.

I climb on top of Evelyn.

Creaaak.

I move down the mattress so our faces meet.

Creaaaaaaaak.

I roll my eyes. Evelyn grins. We hug each other and continue kissing.

Cre, cree, creee, creak.

I pull my lips off of Evelyn and kiss her collarbone. The taste of her salty skin fills my mouth. I move up and begin to bite. I love necking. Evelyn's chest heaves and her hot breath trickles down my shoulder. I grin into the crevice of her neck, sit upright and run my hands across her chest. I slowly pull down her tank-top straps.

Evelyn raises her eyebrows. "You certainly don't waste any time do you?"

I take my hands off her. "Oh. I'm sorry. Do you not want me to?"

"No." Evelyn shakes her head. "Go ahead. You just surprised me, that's all."

Evelyn stretches her arms out on the mattress. I slide one strap down and then the other. I pull down her top and stare at her tiny, milky white breasts. I place my hands over her soft nipples, massage her breasts and kiss her mouth. Evelyn peels off my brown tank top and drops it to the floor. Our hands and mouths wander across each other's bodies. Evelyn grabs my hips and climbs on top again. She presses her crotch against mine. She stops. She stares.

Oh my god. She wants to have sex… I haven't even had sex with a guy.

My muscles lock. Her gaze penetrates.

"Uh…"

"Shut the fuck up." Connor's voice booms through the window. "He actually said he wanted to bang her?"

My eyes dart to the open window. Heavy footsteps kick and crush the gravel of the stone courtyard beneath my window. Students go there on a daily basis to drink beer, smoke cigarettes and disturb me. I can hear everything and anything that is said down there.

"Yup." Andrew's voice climbs the brick wall, spilling into the room. "He was asking me for advice in our room this morning. The guy's such a knob."

Connor bursts out laughing. "Seven Eleven! What an idiot."

Evelyn rolls her eyes. "God, Connor is fucking everywhere," she mutters. "I can't believe Katika likes him."

Connor is the alcoholic-in-residence at Matteoli. He's a student from the University of Western Ontario. Connor plans on getting shitfaced every single night in Italy. Thirty-five nights of binge drinking. He's kept to his record so far. Thirteen days.

I laugh. "Yeah, I know. He's really loud, eh?"

Evelyn smiles down at me. "Anyways, back to what we were doing." She leans over and kisses me.

"Evelyn…" I whisper.

"Yeah?" Evelyn's damp hair falls across her face.

I bite my lip. "Is it alright if we wait till Cinque Terre?"

"Yeah!" Evelyn blinks. "Of course! Totally."

"Are you sure?" I look at her. "That's all right?"

"Yeah." She shakes her head. "It's totally fine."

My shoulders relax. "Okay, cool."

Evelyn lies down beside me, kisses my shoulder and rests her head on my breast.

"What a dumb fuck." Connor's voice fills the room. "Who the hell buys a cooler at a bar?"

"Jeez." I mutter. I climb off the bed and shut the window, muffling the voices.

Evelyn sighs. "Thank you."

"You're welcome." I wrap my arms around Evelyn and glance up at the wooden ceiling beams. I smile. Her small body fits perfectly against my chest. It feels like I've been waiting years to hold rather than be held. Guys always want me to cozy up to their tight pecs and hard abs.

I press my face into her arms.

Mmm. So soft.

"I really like your hips." Evelyn caresses my jutting hip bones.

"What? Really? They're so boney. Look at them, they pop out."

Evelyn strokes my stomach. "I think it's sexy." She runs the tips of her fingers across my stomach. It tickles, in more ways than one.

"Oh." I chuckle. "Well, then. That works out for me."

Evelyn traces outlines on my breasts and biceps, leaning in close.

Wow. Women are so affectionate. Am I being cold by just holding her?

I start running my fingers across her shoulders and arms.

"Mm. So you know Sonia, right?"

"Um." My abs clench. I examine the veneer peeling off the slanting ceiling beams as a distraction. "Yeah, you've mentioned her before."

"She seems pretty butch, right? Do you get any gay vibes from her?"

What the hell?

"Um, no. I've never met her."

"Sure you have." Evelyn looks up at me. "The one in your History of Sport class. Blonde, big shoulders, smiles a lot."

"Ohhh," I sigh. "Sonia. I thought you meant your Sonya."

"Oh, god no." Evelyn frowns and shakes her head. "The blonde one."

Evelyn's Sonya is the 35-year-old lesbian she had started to date a couple of weeks before leaving for Siena. "Age doesn't matter when two people feel a certain way about each other," she had said. The first few days here, Evelyn read aloud cute snippets from Sonya's emails in the common room. I figured I had no chance. That stopped shortly after Sonya began counting down the days until Evelyn's return in her Facebook status. Once I told Evelyn I had a thing for her, she stopped mentioning Sonya altogether.

I draw a circle on Evelyn's shoulder blade. "Oh, well I dunno. Sonia seems straight to me in class, she's just a bit manly. She is an athlete though."

Evelyn kisses my breast. "Yeah, that's true."

Our skin cools. I rest my head on Evelyn's dark hair.

I guess we're gonna' be here awhile.

"Are you comfortable?" I ask.

"Yeah, are you?"

"Yup."

Evelyn smiles and pulls herself closer to me. She talks about her ex-girlfriends, her experiences with different drugs and how excited she is to spend the weekend in Cinque Terre. It's one of the few places in Italy she didn't see when she travelled here with her family three years ago. I hold her close and I listen.

Chapter 6: Cinque Terre

Coast lights illuminate red, blue and green boats knocking against each other in the cool ocean current. A docking ramp rises out of the inky black water, merging into the first of many steep and winding cobblestone streets. Lights glow from open windows and clothes dangle on lines strung across balconies. The warm air, brushing past our bodies smells of salt and fish.

Rio Maggiore lies off the coast of southern Italy. It is one of five villages situated along a section of the Italian Riviera known as Cinque Terre. The area's renowned turquoise waters, rocky coasts and brightly painted towns made it a must-see destination for me.

We had spent our afternoon at the town's main beach covered in small rock boulders and large flat stones. The dazzling turquoise water swept in and out across the shoreline as we adjusted the rocks digging into our backs poorly cushioned by thin towels. We dozed, swam, drank beer, smoked cigarettes and snacked on salty prosciutto, sweet figs and freshly baked bread from a nearby market. As I lay down, Evelyn peaked out from underneath the white towel shielding her eyes from the bright sun and kissed me when no one was looking. We later dined at a restaurant overlooking the ocean that served seafood pasta, chilled white wine and homemade tiramisu. As the sun waned, so too did Evelyn's bashfulness around our friends, the darkness seeming to provide a cloak for our affections.

We sit atop a high ledge, our legs dangling above the slippery docking ramp below. I slide my arms around Evelyn's waist, the warmth of Vodka Pêche putting me at ease. Evelyn squeezes my thigh and leans her head against my temple. Amanda winks at us. My eyes wander to the other side of the small harbour. Tall stucco buildings painted in pastels of pink, yellow and orange cling to the rocky strip of land that sinks into the dark sea and tiny white stars dot a clouded sky. Evelyn's black-painted toenails and tattooed feet sway in the breeze. She nestles her head against my neck and sighs. I pull her closer.

***

Alex whirls around a small, empty square guarded by a wrought iron fence. A fountain, digging into the cobblestone floor, gurgles in the dark, the moonlight shimmering on its surface. We found this place after leaving the harbour and meandering through a wide tunnel painted in colourful graffiti that connects to a series of staircases leading back into the maze of houses and streets. We sit on wooden benches laughing at this evening's entertainment: our friend, Alex. Our shouts disturb the quiet of the sleeping town.

Alex closes her eyes, twirls her hands and sings a French pop song. "Dash-e-mon, tut tut oui."

Katherine laughs, clapping along. "At least she stopped yelling in Serbian."

"Did you figure out what she was saying?" Evelyn asks.

"No, not really. Serbian is pretty different from Hungarian." Katherine scrunches the tiny curls of her hair. "All I know is that she's upset that no one can understand her."

Amanda pouts. "Poor Alex. No one can understand her foreign ways. It's okay Alexxy." She mocks in a baby voice.

I smirk, take a swig of Vodka Pêche and pass the frosted bottle to Evelyn. She pushes it away. I stretch over her and shake the bottle in front of Zykima. "Come on, you're not nearly drunk enough, Miss Seventeen."

"La-la-la, la-la-la." Alex dances in circles across the cobblestone, swaying like a drunken sailor.

Zykima smiles at me with crooked teeth. "Stop trying to get me drunk, Mary!" She squints at me. "First, all that wine at the Contrada dinner. Now this? I'm only supposed to be drinking half as much as you." She wags her finger at me.

I laugh, raising my arms in defense. "Yeah, I know. And I am. Look." I take a gulp of the sweet, cold liquor. Then another. I raise my eyebrows and hold the bottle in front of her. "Your turn."

Zykima shakes her head and takes a small sip. "Maddddy?" I nod in her direction.

Amanda leers, squinting at the bottle in her hand. "Why, thank you Mary." Her lips curl into a smile. I lean back on the bench and squeeze Evelyn's waist.

Katherine holds out the empty bottle, her mouth agape. "Ze Pêche Vodka! Iz all gone!"

"Oh, no!" I shout. "Where's the other bottle?"

Alex stops dancing. "What?" she slurs and stumbles over to Katherine. She yanks the bottle from her hand and brings it to her lips. Drops of Vodka Pêche drip down the side of her mouth.

Evelyn frowns. "We left it in the fridge hostel to chill."

"Oh, fuck. You're right. Let's go back then." I stand up. "I think Alex is done dancing."

"More vodkaaa," Alex trills. She runs ahead, skipping down the stairs. "Ai-tut-tut, la-la-la."

I grin, laughing. "Maybe not. I've never seen her this drunk before!"

Evelyn squeezes my hand. "Well, there's a first time for everything."

I smile and lay a light kiss on her lips and lead her through the square.

The humid air makes the steep, narrow street leading to our hostel that much harder to climb. The bustling restaurants, grocery stories and cafés open during the day are now closed for the night.

The only place still open is a bar named Li Ciavo, where two guys and a girl smoke on the patio. We still haven't found much of a party scene here. Alex begged us, particularly me, to hop on the train to the neighbouring town of Monterosso to go clubbing for the night. We considered picking up a pack of Red Bull energy drinks and staying up all night to catch the 5 a.m. train back to Rio Maggiore, but no one could be bothered.

Evelyn pulls out the key as we reach the entryway leading to our hostel. "I can grab the liquor. You guys wait here."

"I'll come with you." I offer.

"Mmm kay'." Evelyn smiles.

Katherine raises her eyebrows. "Make sure to come back!"

I laugh. "We will, we will! Don't worry."

I follow Evelyn up the zigzagging stone staircases. The neighbourhoods here are hilly mazes. The streets are so narrow and long, and the houses so tall and closely condensed, that it's hard to tell where a street ends and begins.

Evelyn waits for me at the second level of an open street. We smile and kiss deeply. I slip my hand underneath her purple T-shirt and run my tongue along hers. The familiar tingling shoots through me. Evelyn pulls away and saunters ahead of me in a tight navy blue skirt and white tank top. Her wavy black hair cascades down her back. I grab her hips from behind. "God, why do you have to smell so good? You're killing me."

Evelyn swivels, blushing. "Really? You think I smell good?"

"Are you kidding me?" My eyes widen. "You smell amazing. And I love it when you wear your hair like that."

I stare into her eyes and lean in. Evelyn touches her hair and smiles. She turns and jogs up the steps. She opens the green painted door of our two-storey hostel. Light pours out onto the street, illuminating her porcelain skin. She disappears inside.

I find Evelyn standing beside the door, by the staircase leading to the group bedroom occupying the second floor. I shut the door behind me. We slide our arms around each other and kiss and caress underneath our clothes. I grab Evelyn and pull us back against the wall. She presses against me. I grab her neck and pull her lips to mine, savouring their warmth. Evelyn kisses my neck and pulls back. I exhale.

"Wow." Evelyn shakes her head and opens her eyes.

"Yeah." I pant, looking up towards the staircase. Our group room is empty tonight.

"We should grab the vodka, they're waiting." Evelyn steps into the kitchen and opens the freezer door. I stare after her. She pulls out a frosted bottle.

"Oh." I shake my head. "Right."

Dazed, I grab the plastic cups and a 1Lbottle of water sitting on the kitchen table. Evelyn spins around to kiss me and locks the door behind us. We walk close to each other, our hips lightly bumping as we clamber back down to the stone archway opening onto the main street.

"Took you long enough!" Katherine shouts.

"Yeah, yeah. Here's your vodka!" I drop the bottle into Katherine's arms. She stands up and curtsies. "Grat-zee-eh." We made so many jokes about Katherine's poor Italian in our first week that she started mispronouncing words on purpose. I sit on the cold cobblestone in front of the bench, leaving the last seat for Evelyn.

Alex's head droops. "Murrry!" Alex snaps her head up.

I smile. "Hey, Alex. How you doing there?"

"Bad! No one underschtands be."

I chuckle. "It's okay, Alex. I brought you some more vodka."

"Finally, somebody does something right." Alex grabs the bottle and takes a large gulp.

I glance down the empty street. A couple in their mid-twenties strolls toward the harbour, holding hands. I glance at Evelyn. She talks with Amanda.

"Great," I mumble.

I grab the bottle from Alex and take a swig.

We head up to the hostel around 3 am. I slip underneath the sheets of the only double bed in our group room. Alex sleeps beside me, snoring loudly. Evelyn curls up on the single bed in front of me. I glare at Alex in the dark. She took the other half of the double bed I claimed this morning.

I peer over the concrete dock ledge. It drops over thirty feet into frothing seawater washing up against rocks lining the small bay. Further out, sunlight dances and sparkles on the turquoise water, beckoning us to jump in. The sea stretches for countless miles, with nothing but a clear blue sky marking its reach. The coastline we stand on, Cinque Terre, climbs out of its depths. Tourists and locals in bikinis and Speedos crowd the rock-hewn staircase and roped off path behind us.

I squint at Evelyn in the sunlight. "Are you sure you don't want to jump, Evelyn? It's boiling out here."

Evelyn shakes her head and cradles herself back and forth against the rock wall. I look down at the water, then back at Evelyn. Cool water soaked up by my red-and-white flowered bikini top trickles down my stomach. I spot Alex climbing over large rock boulders on her way back up to us. She runs her fingers through her long, wet hair. "What's the matter, Evelyn?"

I purse my salty lips. "She doesn't want to jump. The rocks are freaking her out."

"Oh." Alex nods. "But look at all these people who jumped off. We're all fine. The water's really deep."

Evelyn looks up at us from behind her blue-rimmed, cat's-eye glasses. "I'm just not comfortable doing it, okay? All I picture is blood and bones and ripped limbs when you guys jump. I'm just not cool with it."

"Eeee." I shudder.

"All right." Alex places her hand on her shoulder. "If it really bothers you that much then don't do it. That's totally fine."

"Thank you." Evelyn drags her gladiator sandals across the concrete ground. She hugs her legs and rests her chin on her knees. "Go ahead. I'll be waiting here."

"You can have some of my beer if you like." I point to the two cans of Birra Moretti perched on my biege khaki shorts and towel beside Evelyn.

She shakes her head.

I walk barefoot to the edge of the hot concrete. Amanda, Zykima, and Katherine wave to us, their heads bobbing in the wavy water below. I turn to Alex, water dripping down my face and grin. "Ready?"

"Fuck yeah! Woo!" Alex presses her bare feet into the concrete and leaps.

I laugh and glance back at Evelyn. She averts her eyes, watching tourists walk along the staircase path leading to the rock beach just around the bend. I shrug, take a few steps back, run. and leap off the edge for the third time. Air rushes past me and I plunge into the cool ocean water.

***

I reach across the table for a bottle of Heineken. Evelyn steps into the kitchen. "Great, guess who came to visit? I just got my period." She rolls her eyes and takes a seat.

My shoulders sink.

"Guess I won't be having any fun this weekend." Evelyn grabs a slice of pizza from an open boxon the table. Green peppers and mushrooms melt into the mozzarella cheese. She takes a bite.

"Shitttty." Katherine nods.

Cold, fizzy Heineken fills my mouth. I set the bottle down. "Really shitty."

Alex, Amanda and Zykima join us at the table for dinner. We devour five boxes of pizza and guzzle four 1Lbottles of Heineken and a bottle-and-a-half of melon vodka. We play the drinking games Kings, Shoot 'Em and Charades. Evelyn stops moaning about her cramps. We head outside for a smoke and to escape the sweltering kitchen. We climb onto the roof across from our hostel and slip underneath the shaky, wooden guard rail. Katherine passes me our box of Glamour cigarettes and continues talking to Alex.

The view up here is pretty great. We're high up enough to look over top the layers of pastel buildings to the rolling hills covered in dense greenery and sheer rock. The darkness of the ocean and sky meld together so perfectly that I can barely tell the two apart, save for the moonlight reflecting off the water.

I take a drag of my slim cigarette.

41

"What do you mean the sex was meh?" Katherine scrunches her nose.

Alex leans against the rickety wooden rail. "It wasn't that great. I mean I was a little drunk, but still. He just didn't do much for me."

"If I had a nickel for every time I heard that." Evelyn smirks. "I'm telling you guys, women do it better."

Katherine laughs. "Well, that doesn't give me much hope."

"Don't you wish you were a lesbian now, Katherine?" Amanda winks. "It's not too late to switch you know."

"Ha! Maybe I will! We're always hanging out with girls anyways."

"I think everyone should try having sex with a woman." Evelyn raises her voice so everyone can hear her. "Even if you're straight, it's an important experience. Just to know what a woman feels like."

"Uh, please. I already know what a woman feels like." Alex grabs her breasts.

Amanda chuckles. I pass my cigarette to Evelyn. She takes a drag and holds the burning cigarette between her fingers. "Sex is different. I'm just saying, if you had sex with a guy and you weren't into it, maybe you're not straight."

Alex rolls her eyes. "Look, just 'cause everyone on this trip is a lesbian or bisexual or bicurious, doesn't mean I am. I like giving blowjobs, I like penis. I just need to sleep with a better guy."

I cringe at the thought of giving a guy a blowjob.

Evelyn raises her hands defensively. "I'm just saying."

"Just because Mary might be a lesbian, doesn't mean I am too."

"Alex!" I shout.

"What? Jesus, why is everyone so moody tonight?" Alex puts out her cigarette. "I'm going inside."

Evelyn raises her eyebrows. "Someone's awfully defensive considering she's so sure she's straight."

"There's too much estrogen around here." Amanda stands up. "I think it's getting to her."

"Yeah." I nod. "She just wants to find a guy to hook up with."

Evelyn sets her eyes on me. "I wouldn't be so sure about that." She flicks her cigarette off the roof and steps inside.

"Um, what was that?"

Amanda shrugs. "Don't ask me."

Alex lies down on the double bed again tonight. Evelyn makes a joke about sneaking in beside me before we shut the lights off. I consider crawling into her bed. Neither of us has the balls to follow through. Alex snores beside me the entire night.

I glare.

Chapter 7: Evelyn, Alex and a Bottle of Red

I stroll into the foyer of the former insane asylum now used by the University of Siena for lectures and office space. "History of Italian Sport" taught by dull and sweaty Professor Greg McCoy has just ended. A group of students exit the elevator at the end of the hall. Voices echo and bounce off of the high ceilings of this seemingly ordinary building. There are no traces of its former occupants save for the ghoulish block letter text chiseled onto the stone archway of the main entrance: OSPEDALE PSICHIATRICO. The classrooms upstairs are newly renovated, but the main floor and older parts of the building have cracks running through the cement walls, polished stone floors and towering pillars.

I squint to see if I know anyone in the approaching crowd. A short girl with brunette hair slips past the other students. She stares down the corridor at me. "Marrrrrrry!" she squeals.

Evelyn scampers toward me. Her beige canvas bag with a sketch of naked woman stenciled in dark purple bangs against her hips. She grins, throws her arms around me and kisses me. I blink. When I asked Evelyn what she thought about PDA (public displays of affection) on the train ride to Cinque Terre, she looked at me like I was nuts. It wasn't until our return trip home when we fell asleep in each other's arms, oblivious to rude glances from the train conductor and the laughter of teenage boys, that she stopped caring.

I catch her soft, sweet lips with mine just before her feet touch back down on the ground. "Mmm. Your lips taste sweet," I murmur. Evelyn smiles and tosses her fruit-punch juice box into a garbage can. "Oh." I chuckle.

John, a friend of ours from Evelyn and Amanda's English literature class, gapes at us from the end of the hallway. His bright blue eyes are glued to our faces. More of the guys approach, their heads swiveling as they come closer. Amanda strolls up to us.

"Hey, Mary." She smiles coyly. "You two have all the guys staring you know."

Evelyn rolls her eyes. "Ugh, whatever." She pulls her bag strap over her shoulder. "Are we ready to go?"

"Yeah man." I nod. "Let's get out of here."

The three of us slide on our sunglasses and hop down the stone steps. Volkswagens, Fiats, BMWs, Citroens and Peugeot motorcycles park on the dusty cobbled road. I slip my hand into Evelyn's. She squeezes mine.

"Aw, you guys are adorable." Amanda gushes.

I blush and look past the road at the valley filled with vineyards, cypress trees and farm fields. Tuscan country stretches for miles outside of the city walls. All roads slope toward the edge of the city. It's a twenty-minute trek to our residence from here, all uphill.

The air conditioning that chilled me inside soon gives way to the warm sunlight enveloping our bodies. We stop by a bakery for a breakfast of croissants and espresso before heading back to residence. Evelyn tells me how excited she is for tonight.

***

"Why do you need the whole night? What are you gonna' do for four hours?" Alex glares at me from behind her brown plastic framed glasses.

I shuffle on the floor, bashful. "Well..."

Alex folds her arms over her chest. "Ugh. Fine, but I don't see why you can't come out after you two have your 'alone' time." Alex forms mock air quotes with her fingers.

"Look, I already told you…"

"Mary. We've barely partied this whole trip. The Barone Rosso has been closed for over a week now. I'm sick of Siena."

"Alex," I plead. "Come on. You know we haven't had much time to ourselves. I'll party with you on the weekend."

"Whatever. Just forget it." Alex rolls her eyes and stomps down the hallway. Her flip-flops smack the tiled floor.

"Women!" I mutter.

I slam my door.

***

Evelyn wears her hair down tonight, black and wavy, a single streak of blonde falling across her face. The diamond Monroe stud above her upper left lip sparkles. I grasp the dark glass bottle of Chianti sitting on her nightstand. Evelyn's single dorm is similar to mine, but smaller and narrower, with a desk, window, bed and shelf all to herself, for a few hundred dollars more. I uncork the half-empty bottle and fill Evelyn's green plastic cup.

"Thanks, Mary." Evelyn takes a sip.

"You're welcome." I lean forward and kiss her wine soaked lips.

I settle back against the wall and stretch my legs. I catch Evelyn looking at me. Her lips part, then close. She takes another sip.

I chuckle. "What is it?"

"Nothing," she shakes her head.

"Come on. Tell me."

"Okay." Evelyn places her cup on the nightstand. "I don't want to make a big deal of it, but I thought I'd mention it just so that you're aware."

"Okay?"

Evelyn jiggles her Monroe piercing back and forth with her tongue. "I don't know if it's the best friend thing or what, but…" She takes a deep breath. "I think Alex likes you."

"What?" I laugh. "Oh, come on." I set my cup on the nightstand. "Alex? Why would you say that?"

"Don't you think it's strange that she got so upset as soon as she found out we were spending the night together? Alone?" Evelyn leans forward.

I shrug. "She's just mad 'cause we're all going on field trips this week. We won't really get to hang out 'til next week."

"Okay, but we just got back from Cinque Terre. And there's the whole bed thing." Evelyn's forehead creases. "I mean, it's not like we were going to fuck in front of everyone, but it would have been nice to cuddle at night."

A playful smile passes my lips. "Yeah, that's true." I take a sip of wine. "But I don't think she did it on purpose. She just wasn't thinking. Besides, I should have said something. I just didn't want things to be awkward."

"Okay fine, but I still think she has a thing for you. Everyone else is cool with us hanging out by ourselves, but she wants to do everything with you." Evelyn's eyes widen.

"Hmm. That is true." I purse my lips. "But, I dunno'. I really don't think she's gay."

Evelyn raises her eyebrows, unconvinced.

"Okay, okay. I'll keep an eye on it. I'm kind of curious now."

Evelyn smiles. "I just thought I'd let you know. I don't feel threatened or anything and you're not my girlfriend so it's not really my place." Evelyn peers at me, hesitating. "But I am a bit jealous."

I grin and run my eyes over her body. Her faded blue jean shorts cling to her thighs and her black bra shows underneath her white undershirt and her wavy black hair cascades down her neck and chest. "Well, you don't have anything to worry about. We're friends. I just don't see her that way." I shake my head. "Jeez, why is everyone so into me here? First Mario. Now Alex."

Evelyn stares at me. "Um 'cause you're hot and everyone knows it."

I bite my lip. "You're the one that's hot." Evelyn smirks and crawls towards me. I lean back on the pillow and take her with me. She pinches my neck with her teeth. I laugh. "Trying to get me back for that hickey I gave you?"

"Yes! That bruise was there for three days!"

I kiss her neck. "Haha, do your worst. I don't bruise easily."

Evelyn bites, hard. I exhale. She digs her fingers into my back. We roll around until I'm on top. I kiss her lips and tuck her black bangs behind her ear. "This really sucks," I whisper.

"I know." Evelyn sighs. "It's really shitty luck."

"Honestly, what are the odds of both of us getting our periods on the same weekend?"

"I told you, it's weird! I've only ever had that happen with my best friend. Once!"

I smile. "Somebody's laughing at us."

"At least somebody's laughing." Evelyn rolls her eyes and kisses me. Her hands wander across my body, leaving their mark.

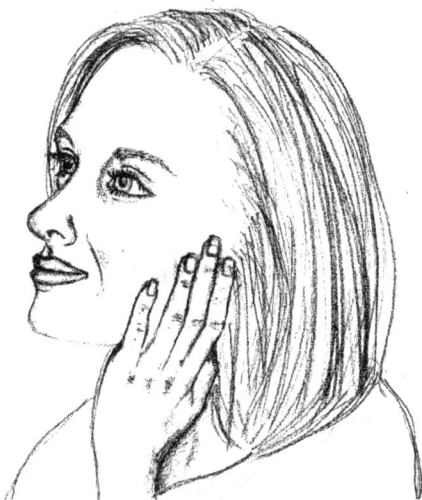

Chapter 8: Awake, But Still Dreaming

I pass my hands over my lips to conceal the incessant smiling. Warm sunlight floods our simple classroom furnished with about thirty single desks, a lectern and wall-mounted chalkboards at the front. The heat rises with the sun every day in Siena, cooling only when dusk falls. Our bodies are kept cool by the central air conditioning in Ospedale Psichiatrico. We are not so fortunate in the residences where students often stick their heads in freezers and stand in front of open fridges for a respite from sticky afternoons. I blush for the seventh time this morning, thinking of her. I can't help it. I've never recalled romantic memories this vividly or frequently. The smoothness of her skin, the touch of her lips, her teasing smile and deep, feminine voice; it envelops me like a crystal clear dream. A dream I do not want to wake up from.

Tricia catches me day dreaming with a pen resting in my hand and whispers, "This guy kills me. Aren't you taking notes?"

"Hmm? Oh." I chuckle. "No. He keeps giving me A's on my papers. I don't see the point."

Her mouth drops. "Are you serious? I got a B on my last one."

"That's not bad." I shrug.

"Yes, it is. I'm a commerce student and this is my last year remember? This is supposed to boost my GPA. I thought this was a bird course."

It is....

I glance at Professor McCoy who is sweating buckets today despite the air conditioning. The daily sweat stains on his golf shirts remind me of the inkblots used for Rorschach psychology tests. Their contracting formations are the most interesting part of his lectures. His voice drops to a dull whisper at the back of class, just the way I like it. Today he graces us with a riveting account of the use of wagons to transport goods in ancient Rome.

Connor turns around and whispers. "Just make sure all your quotes are from the readings and you'll get an A. I've been getting them too."

I smile at Connor and turn to Tricia. "See?"

"What the hell Connor, you never take notes and you're hungover right now!"

"So what? We're on vacation. Lighten up, Tricia. You're over thinking this." Connor turns around and continues his sketch of a dragon climbing a castle. He's actually pretty smart when he's not wasted. We even held down a conversation the other day when he walked me back from class one afternoon.

Tricia scoffs and shoots Connor a dirty look.

"Look, I'll help you with the next one okay?" I offer.

"Alright Thanks. Here's my room number." Tricia scribbles Rm 58 on my notebook.

McCoy releases us for a break ten minutes later, at the halfway mark of class. Students crowd the hall to use the bathroom and stretch their legs. They line up at vending machines to buy espresso, bottled water, chocolate wafers and cornettas filled with chocolate or apricot jam for 75 cents.

Mandy, a recent acquaintance who has asked to room with Tricia and I on the next class trip, spots me leaning against the wall near the fountains. I rip off the packaging of a chocolate cornetta and take a bite.

"Hey, Mary." She smiles.

"Hey, Mandy. How's it going?"

"It's okay, but the lecture is really boring today."

I laugh. "Yeah, I know. I can't take much more of this guy."

"How'd you do on the last assignment?"

"Um, good. I got—" I cut myself off in time. "I did well." I smile.

"I got a B." She fans her face with her hand. "I hope I do better on the next one."

"I'm sure you will."

Mandy and I mosey down the hall. Class starts in a few minutes.

"So, for our trip is there anything in particular you want to see?" Mandy asks. "Because I want to go to the leather market in Florence because I need to buy my boyfriend a belt and then I want to check out…"

As we approach the English Lit class, Evelyn steps out, chatting with another student. My steps falter. She tucks her black hair behind her ears, smiles politely at her friend and opens a bottle of water. I smile.

God, she looks beautiful.

She continues to walk in my direction. I push myself forward, unable to peel my eyes from her face.

"… And I'm pretty sure Tricia wants to see…"

Evelyn looks up. She blinks and does a double-take. A grin slowly spreads across her face, widening as she walks closer. I bite my lip and smile back. We whisper "hey" as our arms brush, our eyes nailed to each other. We turn in unison to catch a glimpse of the other walking away, our grins marking us as fools.

My cheeks flush as we enter the classroom.

"So how does that sound?" Mandy asks as we take our seats.

I sigh. "Amazing."

Chapter 9: I Can Do Casual

At 9 p.m., I wrap my arms around Evelyn. We sit on her bed in Room 32. *Death in Venice*, *The Passion*, *The Talented Mr. Ripley* and *A Farewell to Arms* lay stacked on the white wooden desk. A warm breeze wafts through the open window.

"I really like this song. Listen to the credits." Evelyn wears tight black shorts, an army green tank top and that scent of hers. Her thighs sweat against mine. I glance down at her. The Mac computer screen illuminates her pale face and soft features. Ellen Page strolls across the screen. She swings a jug of orange juice at her hips.

"She's totally a lesbian. Look at the way she walks. There's no way she's straight."

I chuckle. "She's gay?"

"Are you kidding me?" Evelyn tilts her head up at me. "Ellen Page? You didn't know she was gay?"

"Well, I kind of figured from what I've heard. But no, not really."

"Wow, Mary. You really need to up your gaydar."

I laugh. "So I've been told."

I run my fingers across the taut green fabric covering Evelyn's belly button ring. She turns around and kisses me. We spend the next hour and a half making out. Juno plays in the background.

***

I lean my head on Evelyn's soft, damp hair and breathe in the scent of lavender and vanilla. My arm stretches across her shoulders and I close my eyes.

We had fallen into a sleepy silence after too much wine and numerous questions about each other's childhoods, families, past romances and hopes for the future. Evelyn dug deeper and deeper as the night unfolded, as if she was trying to slowly and carefully unwrap an elusive package. The more I divulged, the more anxious I became. I knew it was time to ask the one question I had been avoiding since we met.

"So." I clear my throat. "I didn't want to bring this up, but... I just want to make sure we're on the same page."

Evelyn lifts her head off my chest. "Okay..."

My fingers stroke her pale, soft shoulder.

Just ask her...

I take a deep breath.

"Should I be treating this as a fling?"

Evelyn blinks. "Um, yes."

My breathing hitches. I stare out the window.

"Is that okay with you?"

Her words bite into me. My eyes trace the wide, curving strokes of green, red and yellow paint that spell SONYA on the white paper banner resting on Evelyn's shelf.

"Mary?" Evelyn looks up at me.

"Yeah," I mutter, my voice dry. "That's what I figured." My arm slips off her shoulder. I lay it awkwardly across the mattress behind us. "I just wanted to know how I should be treating this, is all." I force a smile. "Now I know."

My eyes sting underneath dry contacts. Evelyn paid a local artist fifteen Euros to personalize the banner.

"But..." Evelyn grasps my thigh. "I'm not opposed to getting to know you. I do like you."

"What?" I pretend not to hear her.

Evelyn raises her voice. "I still want to get to know you. I don't know about you, but I'm not in this just for sex. I could masturbate if I wanted to get off. I like you. I think you're really cool."

"Yeah." I nod. "Well, same here." I slide my sweaty thigh away from hers. "I don't even know if I want a relationship. It's way too soon to tell. I just thought I'd bring it up so that I know for sure." The words tumble out of my mouth. "You know? To cover my bases. I waited too long with the last guy I was seeing."

Matt and I saw each other for three months. We flirted, texted, chatted on MSN and watched movies in his basement from midnight to 5 a.m. on weeknights. When I asked him to take me out on a real date, he told me he couldn't handle commitment right then, even though he liked me.

"For sure, I totally get that. I really do want to keep spending time with you. I like to take the time to get to know people." Evelyn traces spirals on my stomach. "And I'm not just going to ignore you after this. I'm sure we can keep hanging out in Toronto."

"Yeah." I nod. "For sure. I'm the same way. Like with people. I actually like getting to know them. And I don't sleep around. Obviously. Haha. You know I'm still a virgin."

Evelyn walks her fingers across my stomach. "Not for much longerrr."

My eyes widen.

"Wow." Evelyn turns on the mattress. "I'm sorry. I didn't mean it like that."

I chuckle nervously. "No, don't be silly. It's totally fine."

"Okay, good." Evelyn pecks me on the lips. She rests her head on my stomach.

My thoughts wander back to Matt. It took me two months to get over him and we only made out a few times. It was the closest I had gotten to a relationship since a few casual boyfriends in high school whose attempts at sex always failed. I had since gotten used to fooling around with guys at parties and bars, but that's because I barely knew them.

***

I follow Evelyn out of the kitchen at 3 a.m. She flicks the light switch off and hops the two steps leading into the empty common room. She turns and draws closer, smiling. "I really like this set-up. We're kind of creating our own label."

I grab her waist. "Hmm, that is true, isn't it? Who needs labels?"

"Exactly." Evelyn throws her arms around my neck and kisses me. "I'll see you when you get back from Venice?" Evelyn dangles her key.

"Yeah." I nod.

""kay, cool. Have a good trip."

"Thanks. Good night."

Evelyn climbs the stairs to the third floor. I watch her until she disappears around the corner. I slink past closed doors and damp clothing hanging on white laundry racks.

You can totally do this, Mary. Just keep it casual.

I nod to myself as I slowly pull the latch handle on my Room 23. I smile. Kirsten left the light on for me as usual.

Chapter 10: Venice: A City for Lovers

The lobby of Hotel Ariel Silva is dim with soft lighting. It is small, well-furnished and clean. It is going to cost us. Tricia strides up to the desk and brushes the hair away from her eyes. Natasha hovers beside me, waiting.

The man at the desk nods. "I check, I check. One minute."

I hoist my backpack straps to alleviate the pain pulsing in my tight shoulders, dampened by sweat. I've crammed in enough clothes and toiletries to last me five days. I check my watch. It's almost midnight. The man returns to the desk, frowning. "I sorry miss. We have no rooms."

"Fuck," Natasha mutters.

"Nothing?" Tricia squeaks.

"No, I sorry."

"Grazie." Tricia grabs the handle of her suitcase and drags it to the door. Natasha and I exchange a look and follow her out onto the street. This is the fifth hotel we've scouted with no available rooms.

We had glided into one of the eastern ports of Venice on a vaporetto water taxi when the sun was setting, draping a shimmering curtain of light on the city. We snapped photographs of ourselves on the boat, with the world famous city behind us. I knew I had made the right choice to visit Venezia, a city built of water canals and narrow alleys and historical churches. Why would I have second-guessed coming here? That was over four hours ago. None of us thought to book a hotel in advance. None of us knew where the hell we were going. Arriving in the one of the most beautiful cities in the world after being dragged through museums and historical sites in Mantua, Ferrara and Verona for three days with classmates I didn't care for was not romantic or adventurous. Venice had transformed into a twisting maze of dark alleys, polluted waterways and expensive shops and restaurants within hours.

"Well, where do we go now?" Tricia huffs.

"We keep walking." I sigh. "There's bound to be a hotel somewhere in this damn city."

"Why don't we just pay the extra money and go to the hotel the other class stayed at?" Natasha suggests. "The English Lit one? They left this morning. The rooms should be available."

Figures we'd end up in the hotel she just left.

The last three days away from Evelyn had given me more and more time to admit that I wasn't okay with what she had told me. It was all I could think about, but I had no idea what to do. All I knew was that I wasn't happy about it.

"Fine," I mutter. "Let's go."

The city map we grabbed at the last hotel is useless in our hands. Streets end without warning, signs lead in all directions and none of the streets are straight. We get lost seven times, even after calling our classmate Mandy for directions. How does one find their way in a city designed for people to get lost in? Persistence and blind luck. After cursing Venice for the tenth time, we stumble down an alleyway leading to a hotel that looks like every other hotel. Luckily, it is finally the right one.

***

Venice is hot. Really, fucking hot. I was warned about the extreme daytime temperatures in Italy in the dead of August. I thought I had adjusted to the heat in Siena. But in Siena, there is shade. In Siena, I have a permanent room close by where I can lie on the bed and guzzle water. In Siena, the heat feels dry. Venice is swarming with tourists gawking at street vendors and shops pedaling so-called authentic Venetian masks, Murano glass and Marzipan delicacies. Not only is Venice hot, it is humid. The air is ripe with it. I can see haze rippling through the crowds, brushing up against my skin as it slithers past me. I run my hand across my clammy shoulder.

Gross.

A group of American tourists bump into me. I hiss. Tricia and Natasha emerge from the glass shop carrying bags filled with boxes of hand-blown glass objects. The prices are insane. The only gift I've purchased is a pair of blue bulb earrings for my aunt. They cost twenty Euros.

"We haven't seen the docks yet. Do you guys want to go there?" I ask.

"Um, yeah I guess." Lines are etched into the dark bags beneath Tricia's eyes. She wipes sweat from her brow. "But we have to come back. I still have a bunch of souvenirs to buy and I want another mask for my mom."

"Well, we've all seen water before, but okay." Natasha slides her Prada glasses onto her face and adjusts the shiny black leather purse perched on her shoulder. I clench my fists and lead the way.

We spent last night at a club Tricia suggested. The drinks were ten Euros each and I ran out of smokes. I was down to fifteen Euros until I tracked down an ATM or a bank, which I didn't find until this morning. Tricia wanted to get loaded. She hadn't gotten laid the entire trip and was dying to sample the 'local cuisine'. A group of attractive men in their late twenties approached the three of us, but the conversation slowed to a halt after ten minutes of small talk limited to hand gestures and Tricia's poor Italian. She groaned after they excused themselves. Natasha offered us her menthol cigarettes and a round of shots before we called it a night. That, after a day spent shopping.

The Piazza San Marco is beautiful, as is the view of St. Mark's Basilica—which we avoid entering upon seeing the six-hour line—

and so is the view of the ocean. We last about forty-five minutes before the heat drives us back to the shaded streets in the centre of the city. This is the extent of our sightseeing before we plunge into stores again. I leave the girls to return to the hotel. I seek out quiet streets marked by graffiti, with small homes and cool patches of shade. I perk up after seeing an IKEA catalogue lodged between the bars of a black metal gate. I pull out my slim, silver Canon digital camera to take a quick photo to show my friends back home. I haven't thought about home in a while. I've only called my family twice in over three weeks, dodging questions about their theory that I had met a boy who was so distracting I had neglected to call home or email more often. I logged onto Facebook once, to message my best friend to tell her I had met someone. My stomach turns every time I think of her. Like a rusty wrench twisting in my gut.

She doesn't want a relationship. That's fine. Whatever, we just met.

I pull out my city map and follow a zig-zagging path back to the hotel. I haven't exactly conquered Venice, but I can navigate my way around as long as I stay close to the major streets. I swing the backpack from my shoulder, drop my bags in the corner of the hotel room and lie down on the bed. My skin tingles as a blanket of crisp, cool air conditioning wraps around me. I try to nap, but my mind won't let me. I groan and roll off the edge of the bed. I lock the door and head out onto the street. I take a deep breath and try to relax.

I have a few hours to myself now. I can decompress.

I wander alongside a street with two and three storey buildings squished beside each other on either side of the canal; their walls and window shutters are brightly painted but lack the vibrancy of Rio Maggiore. A breeze follows me, tickling my skin. I let out another long breath. I watch a group of young guys and girls hoist their suitcases and bags out of a water taxi stopped a block past my hotel.

We should have thought of that. If we had known where we were going.

They laugh loudly, their eyes devouring the street like it's an edible paradise. I shake my head and step inside of a narrow café painted yellow and furnished with three white metal tables and matching chairs positioned out front. I order a café macchiato and a chocolate cornetta and claim the corner spot facing the street. The women inside speak softly in Italian. A man in his mid-forties sitting one table over looks up from his newspaper and smiles. I nod and smile back. I take a large bite of the flaky pastry and run my tongue along its sweet chocolate centre. I sip on the hot espresso macchiato, the velvety milk foam brushing against my lips. Just like hers.

My stomach sinks.

I don't understand. If she likes me and isn't in this just for sex, then what are we doing? This is like Matt all over again. But, I can't leave her. I've never met anyone like her.

I approach the bar again and ask for a glass of water. Luckily, the woman understands English. I can't remember the word for water right now. I drain the glass, swirling the last of it in my mouth and return to my seat.

Maybe I should go after Leo. I could get him.

I shake my head. I uncross my sweating thighs and lean forward in my seat. I watch the street, running my eyes along the short bridges over the canal, the murky green water, the narrow alleys, the shops across the water and the tourists walking past me. My attempt at forced relaxation does not alleviate the growing tension building in my gut. It sets it on fire. I hop out of my seat and push the chair against the table.

I can't handle two more days travelling with those two in Milan. I have to see her.

I return to the hotel to gather my belongings. I call Mandy's cell phone from the front lobby and catch the morning train with her back to Siena.

Chapter 11: Bitch Sticks

It's Friday night at 11 p.m., week four of the Summer Abroad Program. I walk down the wide, sprawling steps of Matteoli Residence, stop in front of the porter's desk and hand the woman my green lanyard and key. "Grazie," I grunt.

Katherine and Alex stroll past me and veer right at the courtyard. I venture a glance. The shadows of student bodies and the limbs of tall trees shift with my terse movements. Students always go there to chill, smoke and talk. There's no way in hell I'm going there tonight.

"Guys," I call. "Let's go to the park with the playground. Everyone can hear us out there. I want some privacy."

Katherine turns around. "Booo!" she whines.

"There'll be a ton of mosquitoes out there anyways," I grumble. I tread across the black-and-white checker tiled floor of the tall, arching corridor built of stone and concrete. The warm air draws me out into the night. Katherine and Alex follow close behind me, their flips flops clacking noisily on the floor.

61

I close my eyes and exhale.

She had dug too deep. Asked too many questions. Torn into the seam of my personal life. Why did she need to know all those things? There must have been a reason, some sort of motivation. Or was she simply passing the time until I was ready to untangle myself from the web of her?

Fuck her for asking about my siblings, about my past relationships, about where I stand sexually. Yes, maybe I am a lesbian. And yes, maybe I am falling for you. What did she care? I had been pushing for weeks now. Pushing for some indication of what I meant to her. And now I have what I wanted. And now I wish I hadn't asked.

Three men in jeans and T-shirts loiter at the corner of Via dei Rossi smoking cigarettes. The restaurant at the end of the street grows dark. The owner steps out of the doorway and pulls out a pair of keys to close up. I stride faster, hiking the road leading deeper into town. Bright blue and yellow striped Tartuca flags with the tortoise symbol line the crumbling brick walls of the Tartuca Contrada. Students from Matteoli Residence, including myself, have adopted the Tartuca identity during our stay here as guests. Siena is made up of seventeen districts known as contrade, named after their historical symbol or animal represented on their colourful flags hung throughout the town. The Sperandie Residence is only five blocks away, but occupies another contrade, the Civetta or Owl contrade. The flags hang limply on their poles tonight, with no wind to stir their celebratory banners.

The Tartuca Contrade residents were still celebrating their victory in the July Il Palio horse race two weeks after my arrival with U of T. The Piazza Del Campo, located in the heart of Siena, is covered with sand and barricaded twice every summer to host the historical event. A jockey and his horse are selected from ten of the seventeen contrade to race against each other in the burning sun. Hundreds of fans scream and shout from within the cage set up in the centre of the circular race track, or from balconies or rooftops. The victors parade through town in historical garb beating their drums with raised flags, dancing and singing in the streets and cracking open dozens of wine kegs to share. In the nights following the race, locals set up long wooden tables on which to drink wine, devour pasta, boar and tiramisu and sing until 3am. The celebrations are over. The Civetta Owl Contrada won the second race in August.

That day I openly displayed my affection for Evelyn.

That day, our group of friends and I stood on a stone ledge to get a better view of the contrade flag ceremony before the race. I leaned against the brick wall with Evelyn standing in front of me and wrapped my arms around her stomach. "Oh." She chuckled and closed her hands around mine. "I like this. Right in front of the bishop." She pointed at the highest window of the Siena di Duomo church. The black-robed bishop smiled and waved to the pulsing audience in the square below. I rested my chin on Evelyn's shoulder and pulled her closer. Young men dressed in pantaloons and armour dazzled the audience with flag throwing and twirling. My classmate Tricia and her group of friends perched on the ledge across from us whispered and stared.

I didn't care. That was the first time I held a girl in public.

***

"Mary!" Katherine shouts. "Wait up. Our legs aren't as long as yours. Jesus!"

The pebbles of the playground crunch beneath my feet. The vacant swings, teeter-totters and slide cast heavy shadows in the light of tall lampposts. I whirl around. Katherine and Alex catch up to me.

"Mary." Alex stops in front of me, startled. "What the fuck is wrong? Is it Evelyn?"

Katherine peers at me. "Yeah, you don't look so good."

Energy courses through my body despite a daunting physical exhaustion. My shoulders droop and my head aches. "I'm just tired," I grumble. "Come on."

A brick barricade about two feet high surrounds the small park. Four benches overlook the panoramic view of Siena just beyond the wall. Clay shingled houses, shops and buildings glow beneath a dark sky dotted with bright stars and a crescent moon.

I plunk down onto a swing and pull out my pack of Glamours— what we call bitch sticks—long, slim cigarettes that burn twice as fast

63

as regulars, but are smooth on the throat and dainty to hold. Smoke slithers out of my mouth. Katherine and Alex approach the set of swings. I toss my Glamours to Alex.

Katherine pulls out her pack of Diana's and hovers over me. "What's bothering you, Mary?"

Alex leans on the edge of the low brick wall. "Yeah, what the hell happened in Venice? You're acting all weird."

I take a drag. "Nothing happened. I just had a shitty time. I didn't want to be there. You know I don't like travelling with my classmates. I wanted to be here with you guys… and Evelyn, but it was Venice, man, how could I say no?"

"Yeah." Katherine frowns and slides onto the swing beside me. "I don't like my class either. But, even if you had a shitty time, at least you got to see Venice, right?"

"I don't think Venice is that great." Alex picks at the crumbling cement on the brick wall. "There are better cities. Like Prague or Berlin or Paris." She sighs. "God, do I love Paris."

Alex will be starting an eight-month student exchange in Paris starting this October after our stint in Siena. My jealousy runs deep. I've grown fond of this country and the friendships I've formed here. Part of me never wants to return home. Coming out to friends and family is something I could put off for years.

"Nah, it was nice and all that." I ash my cigarette on the ground. "Tricia and that dark-haired girl are just so ditsy. I felt so out of place. They were busy picking up guys all weekend and all I could do was think of her." I sway on the swing, my feet dragging on the ground. My temple throbs. "Did you see her reaction when I came into the kitchen? She just looked at me and asked what I was doing back early. No "It's good to see you." or anything. What the fuck was that?"

"Well what did you want, Mary? You know she doesn't want anything serious, right?" Katherine digs her black Old Navy flip flops into the gravel and pushes off.

"Yeah, Katherine," I mutter. "I know that."

"Is that what she told you?" Alex stands up and toys with the chain links of my swing.

I sigh. "Yeah. When we had that 'date night' before I left for Venice. She told me I should be treating this as a fling and that she doesn't want a relationship right now."

"I knew it." Alex shakes her head. "She's using you. She's just going to go back to that 35-five-year-old when all this is done."

The name Sonya cuts me like a razor.

"You really think so?" I hop off the swing. "She's almost twice her age. I just don't get it."

"She's older, Mary, more experienced." Katherine says. "I think she feels taken care of with her."

I suck on my cigarette. "She's insecure, that's what it is." I jab my finger towards Katherine. "Sonya eats out of the palm of her hand. She loves it."

"I don't know what she wants from an old bat like that," Alex says.

"I don't know what to do." I groan. "I can't sleep with her now. I like her too much." I pace back and forth in front of the swings. "Maybe I should just stop seeing her."

"Yeah, I think that's a good idea," Katherine looks at me. "If she doesn't want anything serious, then just leave it alone."

"No. Fuck that." Alex turns to face me, sidestepping Katherine. "She's full of it, Mary. She can't play it both ways. You're going to be the one that gets hurt. Take control while you can."

I close my eyes for a moment. "That is true. She can't have it both ways. You're either my fuck-buddy or you're my girlfriend." I flick my cigarette over the wall. "If she didn't want anything serious then why has she been pulling all this coupley-crap with me? Being all affectionate and shit, holding my hand and cuddling after we fooled around?"

I press my fingers against my temples to alleviate the building pressure.

"Oh, and that stupid 'date night'?" I yell. "She was being so intimate! The bottle of wine, watching a movie, asking me about my family and who I've dated? We cuddled and made out for like four hours! What the fuck was that?"

Alex crosses her arms and nods reassuringly.

"Mary." Katherine places her arm on my shoulder. "Calm down."

"No." I shove her off. "She can't do this to me. Jerk me around like this. She's playing games with my head."

Alex steps closer. "At least you know now. Turn it around on her. Use her for sex and get your lesbian experience. Just detach yourself."

"Guys…" Katherine's voice shakes.

I ignore her. "You don't think it's too late?"

"No." Alex scowls. "Whenever she's with you, just remember what she's doing to you."

I stare at the empty tables left from the July Il Palio parties. A group of kids run close to the park laughing and shouting. Their parents guide them past us. "Yeah," I whisper. "If she wants to fuck around with me then I'll do the same. I can be cold. I can use her too."

"Just don't let her get to you." I clench my teeth. "I won't."

Katherine stares at me, her eyes wide. I walk away.

Whatever. It's not her heart on the line.

I grasp the rough brick wall and peer out at the city that has felt like home for the past four weeks, at the stars I wanted to fall asleep under with Evelyn. The constellations are different on this side of the world. I'm different on this side of the world.

I've never felt this way before. Not with Matt, not with Ben, not with anyone. The intimacy, the desire. It's just not the same. Guys were so simple, so replaceable.

I shut my eyes to stop any tears.

Alex grabs my shoulder. "Are you okay?"

"Yeah." I nod. "I'm fine. Let's head back."

Alex turns around. "Katherine?" she calls. "Are you coming?"

"Yeah…" Katherine murmurs. "I'll be right behind you."

"Let's go. It'll be all right, Mary." Alex smiles and places her arm around my shoulders. My jaw clenches. I stride ahead of her, my legs swiftly carrying me through the deserted street. I gaze at my distorted shadow stretching across the cobblestone road. My stomach turns. I step inside of Matteoli, squinting at the bright light.

Chapter 12: Gin: The Panty Dropper

Evelyn's hands hover over Amanda's Dell laptop. "What's wrong, Mary? Did something happen in Venice?"

We sit on the blue couches in the common room and listen to Bjork and drink Diet Sprite and gin. According to Evelyn, gin makes girls horny. It's an alcoholic lubricant, the ultimate panty-dropper. The drink she fixes for us tastes like club soda mixed with rubbing alcohol and liquid sugar. I sip on it anyway. I want to invite Evelyn back to my room. It's not the gin talking.

"Yeah, you're here with us now." Amanda sprawls on the cool tile floor. "What is it?"

I shake my head. "I don't wanna' talk about it."

"Maryyy." Evelyn pouts.

I bite down on an ice cube melting in my mouth. "It's nothing. Really. I'm fine."

Evelyn raises her eyebrows. I drink my gin. Amanda stares.

"Here, this'll cheer you up." Evelyn smiles.

Evelyn plays an upbeat indie song I've never heard. Whatever they're playing still sounds like Bjork. My temples burn.

Should I invite her back to my room?

I pull my navy blue basketball shorts up my thighs.

I know I shouldn't.

I slide onto the cool tile floor.

It's always fucking humid in here.

"Feels nice down here, doesn't it?" Amanda smiles.

"Mmm."

Amanda and Evelyn run through their iTunes playlist, gabbing about their favourite indie bands and some hot lesbian artist. I swirl my glass. The ice chunks clink. I think about it one more time.

Fuck it. I haven't seen her in five days.

"Evelyn." I raise my voice. "You wanna' come chill in my room for a bit?"

Evelyn takes her eyes off the screen. "Uh, yeah. Sure. You cool here, Amanda?"

"Yeah, go ahead."

Evelyn passes the Dell to Amanda and runs her hands through her damp hair. My thighs clench. I place my empty glass on a low white table and grab my key. We walk down the hallway to my room. I turn the key. The latch clicks loudly. I push the door open for her. Kristina's still out for the night.

Evelyn sits down on my bed. I shut the door and join her. Our eyes meet. I lean forward and kiss her. I run my hands down her lower back. Evelyn leans back. The weight of her gaze falls on me. "Mary, what is it?"

I glance at her pale thighs. "Nothing," I mumble.

Evelyn rests her head on the crevice of my neck and wraps her soft body around mine. My shoulders stiffen. "Tell me what's wrong." Evelyn whispers. "I'll make it better."

My eyes bore into the white wall and my arms lay limp at my sides. Evelyn's hair rubs my neck. The scent of lavender and vanilla drift into my nose. The knot in my stomach loosens. She sighs and squeezes me. I feel my arms slide around her back and pull her towards me. I close my eyes. The exhaustion of the last five days melts.

"Aw, Mary," Evelyn purrs and kisses my neck.

My eyes snap open.

This isn't why you brought her here.

I grit my teeth. I push Evelyn onto the pillow and push my lips on her. I press against her. Her legs split. I slide between her thighs. Evelyn's eyes widen. "That's a bold move."

"What?" I snap my head back. "It is?"

"Um, yeah. Are you sure you've never done this before?" Evelyn's voice shakes.

I hover over her, my hands digging into the mattress. "Yeah. Why would I lie about that?"

"I dunno." Evelyn lowers her eyes.

I straddle her. I breathe onto her neck. She moans. My lips kiss her again and again. My body moves back and forth over her. Her eyes follow me. I bite her neck and press harder. "Mary," Evelyn breathes into my ear.

"What?" I pant.

"Let's talk. I want to hear about your trip."

I stop. I roll my eyes and collapse onto the mattress. Evelyn leans on her side and pecks me on the lips. She snuggles close. I lay a limp arm across her shoulders and stare up at the wooden ceiling beams. She tells me she's glad that I came back early. She tells me to have a good time in Rome even though I'll be gone for the weekend. We have plenty of time. There's no reason why we need to fuck in Italy. We have Toronto. She leaves me to pack just before midnight. I slam my door once she's out of earshot. Her scent clings to my brown tank top. I pull it off and hurl it at the pile of clothes in my corner of the room. I drop my head into my hands.

"Fuck," I mutter. "It's too late."

Chapter 13: Escape to Rome

The Piazza Navona is a large central square in Rome, Italy. It is made beautiful by ornate, stone-carved fountains of muscular Greek gods from the Renaissance, cobblestone groundwork, gleaming restaurant patios and inviting storefronts. Low-rise buildings surround the square, much like the Piazza Del Campo in Siena. Clusters of tourists swarm the area to rest their weary feet and over-heated bodies with a scoop of creamy gelato, a glass of sparkling San Pellegrino or a slice of freshly baked pizza. Alex and I opt for a seat by a fountain on which to enjoy our double-scoop gelato ice cream cones.

Alex sinks her teeth into the melting heap of pistachio and dark chocolate truffle gelato melting under the rays of the sun. I lay my lips on the soft, creamy layer of melon gelato and moan. Alex chuckles and nods in agreement. I watch chattering tourists rush past us and am grateful that my second trip to Rome has been way more relaxing than my first. No airheaded classmates to drag me out shopping in pursuit of yet another leather satchel, no sweating, gray-haired professor to drone on about the ruins and no thoughts of a first kiss with a beautiful brunette to bewitch me. Just a close friend and I, wandering this mesmerizing city together.

Alex glances at me from behind her aviator sunglasses. "I told you this would be good for you. It's a great city isn't it?"

I sigh and take a moment to absorb the historical urban scene surrounding us. Narrow cobblestone roads pour out of the piazza at multiple points, luring tourists and locals to explore further into this bustling city. Waiters dressed to the nines in pressed white shirts and black vests glide between tables at restaurants and cafés, taking orders and presenting mouth-watering Italian cuisine. Families, couples and tourist groups pose eagerly, grins plastered to their faces for the snap of an everlasting photograph. Children shout and laugh, running around vendor carts scattered throughout the square selling postcards, key chains and bottles of water. I dip my hands and arms into the fountain behind us, rubbing away the sweet, sticky remnants of gelato. I splash the cool water on my face.

"Yeah, it really is. I'm glad I came with you. I think we needed some 'alone time'." I form air quotes with my fingers and wink.

Alex rolls her eyes. "She really is trying to have her cake and eat it too. You do know that right?"

Evelyn had been flitting through my mind for the past two days, forcing me to admit that I was not willing to break it off, even if it meant not getting exactly what I wanted: her, all to myself. Alex has made an amiable distraction, guiding me through the city, from the Spanish Steps, the Pantheon and the Colosseum to the Piazza Navona and the Trevi Fountain. Not to mention afternoons spent indulging in espresso, pastries and cigarettes, and to top it off, evenings drinking Chianti wine, eating pasta linguini and tiramisu, and sipping sweet aperitifs.

Oh, and last night. Last night was wicked. We hit up the Spanish Pub Crawl for the price of 40 Euros. We joined Connor and his hard-core drinking buddies, hitting up two bars and three clubs starting at 9 p.m. and ending at 4 a.m. The Cave was the grimiest. Flashes of bright light flickering every five seconds revealed the sweating bodies of the crowd, who you were dancing up on and where your drink had disappeared to. Alex put the moves on John. She claimed she was just dancing. I grinded up on Leo, going only so far as to suck the salty, sweaty skin of his neck. I even danced with Connor and Andrew. Their stiff bodies and awkward poses were poor substitutes for Evelyn's soft kisses, subtle curves and tight behind. John invited us back to the guys' room at 4 a.m. to keep drinking beer. Alex and I declined and crawled into bed just as we had done in Rio Maggiore. I caught myself wrapping my arm around Alex in the middle of the night thinking she was Evelyn. I flinched, rolled over and drifted back into my dreams of her.

I rub my wet hands up and down the length of my slender arms to cool down. "I dunno'. I think I overreacted. I'll just be careful, more detached when I get back. I'm willing to see where things go. There's obviously something between us." I sit back down beside Alex.

Alex's forehead creases. "Okay, Mary. But, don't say I didn't warn you."

"I'll be fine, stop worrying so much. I just want to enjoy the rest of our trip. Not all of us get to go to Paris after this!" I slap Alex's bicep.

"Hey!" Alex rubs her arm, pretending to be annoyed. "I already asked you to come travel with me before I start in October!"

I cock my eyebrow and grin. "I already told you, I'm not running away with you, Alex."

Alex bats her eyelashes. "A girl can't help but try."

I bump her knee with mine, giggling. "Mmm hmm. No wonder Evelyn is jealous."

Alex laughs. "Whatever, you should thank me. It's making her want you more."

I smirk, remembering how Evelyn crawled on top of me less than a week ago. I can't wait to take her in my arms again and kiss the hell out of her.

Chapter 14: Siena

Alex fries chicken breast and boils mushroom tortellini on the hot plates in Matteoli's kitchen. Behind us lies the dining area decorated with a simple white wooden table, eight metal-framed chairs, an ironing board, a 20-inch television hanging in the corner and an open window overlooking a small courtyard on the ground floor beneath us. The faint breeze rolling in makes the kitchen just bearable.

Beyonce's "Beautiful Nightmare" music video plays in the background on MTV Italia, taunting me.

"Every night I rush to my bed / With hopes that maybe I'll get a chance to see you / When I close my eyes / I'm going out of my head / Lost in a fairytale / Can you hold my hands and be my guide.... You can be a sweet dream or a beautiful nightmare / Either way I don't wanna wake up from you."

I pace the tiled floor and rub my palm along my sweaty neck. "Alex, something is really off here. What do you think happened while we were gone?"

The steam from the boiling water fogs up Alex's glasses. She slides them over her sweaty forehead and stirs the tortellini with a wooden spoon. "Yeah, there's something they're not telling us. I don't know what's up with this Australian chick they met on the weekend."

My eyes narrow.

Evelyn, Amanda and Katherine met Lilith at Ossessione beach this past Sunday while Alex and I were in Rome. Lilith is an exchange student touring Siena for the next three days before she meets up with a friend in Paris. The four of them swapped numbers and promised to meet up for dinner this week.

"Yeah, what the fuck is that about? They keep going on about how great she is." I cross my arms and push my back against the wall. "You think Evelyn's into her?"

"No. She's straight." Alex shakes salt over the boiling water. The chicken sizzles in the frying pan. Oil splatters onto Alex's arm. She yelps and drops the ladle. "Fuck." She hops around the kitchen, clutching her arm.

"Oh, shit." I run over to her. "Are you okay?"

"Goddamnit, Mary. You better fucking eat all this."

I laugh and turn on the faucet. "Every last bit." I motion for Alex to put her arm under the cold water.

Bare feet pad the staircase leading into the kitchen. Amanda pops her head through the doorway. Her short bangs sweep across her forehead. "Oh." She falters. "Hey guys. What's up?"

"Oh. Hey Amanda." I smile. "Just cooking some dinner. Want some?"

"Oh, no thanks." Amanda rubs her belly. "I already ate half a ball of mozzarella and a bunch of tomatoes."

She opens the fridge door and grabs a can of Coke. I glance at Alex. She nods. I slide in beside Amanda. "Hey, do you know where Evelyn is? I've barely seen her all day."

"Uh." Amanda averts her eyes. She presses her finger down on the aluminum tab, puncturing the can. Coke fizzes over the rim.

I step forward. "Be careful with that."

Amanda's cheeks flush. She slurps the cold brown liquid before it hits the floor. "Got it."

"So, have you seen her?"

"Right, yeah. Um, she's out getting gelato with Kirsten and Adriana."

"What?" I step back. "Kirsten?"

"Yep." She nods.

"Are you sure?"

"Mmm hmm."

"Okaaay. Did they say when they'd be back?"

"Uh, no. I wouldn't wait up. You know how good gelato is." Amanda laughs nervously. "Anyways." her voice cracks. "I'm gonna' head back to my room. Catch you guys later." Amanda waves and scales the staircase in one quick step.

I turn to Alex. "Okay, what the fuck was that? Has everyone gone batty?!"

"I know. Everyone's avoiding us. Since when do Evelyn and Kirsten hang out?" Alex points to the ninety-nine cent Chardonnay I bought for cooking. "Open that wine bottle for me."

"I know right?" I press the metal corkscrew into the bottle and twist. "Why is Evelyn out with my roommate?" I yank on the cork.

Pupt.

"I need to figure out what's going on. This is bullshit. Everyone's ignoring us. Evelyn wouldn't even look at me earlier when I said hi."

Alex nods and pours the wine over the chicken. "Let's ask Amanda and Katherine if they want to come to the Campo tonight."

"Yeah, I want to find Evelyn." I grab the bottle and take a swig.

"Whoa, whoa. I thought that was for cooking."

"Whatever. I need to mellow out." I grab a plastic cup from the cupboard. "Here, I'll be civilized about it." Alex laughs and drains the tortellini.

***

The Piazza Del Campo is beautifully eerie at night. Siena's town square is carved out like a massive oyster shell covered in fading red brick. The Palazzo Publico, the town hall and former castle, and the Torre del Mangia, the tower, loom at the head of the square. Tall buildings with glowing windows surround the square, pressing against each other, and streets and neighbourhoods branch out from here, the centre of town. Restaurants, cafés, souvenir shops and wine stores operate on the first floor, housing and rental space on the levels above. Hundreds of people sprawl on the ground in groups drinking wine, smoking cigarettes and eating pizza. Patrons willing to pay a ten Euro sitting fee lounge in the patio chairs of restaurants with jacked-up prices aimed at tourists. They sip Chianti wine and dip freshly baked bread in olive oil and balsamic vinegar while they wait for their first course of antipasto.

I wedge my bottle of cheap chardonnay between my legs and scan the crowded Campo.

Forget it. There's no way I'll spot her. She's probably not even here.

I take a sip. Students from our program sit cross-legged in a massive circle playing the drinking game Kings; cards are positioned face down and flipped at each turn to indicate the amount of drinks to be handed out or which game to be played.

Katherine digs through her purse, looking for cigarettes. Amanda watches her, waiting, tightly gripping her bottle of Chianti. Katherine retrieves a pack and nods to Amanda. They stand up simultaneously.

Alex looks up. "Where are you guys going?"

"We're gonna' head back and watch a movie or something." Amanda smiles.

"But, we just got here," I say.

"We're tired." Katherine covers her mouth and pretends to yawn. "We're just gonna' head back."

"Here, we'll come with you." I stand up and wipe the dirt off my Capris. "Nothing's going on here anyways."

"No, no." Katherine motions for me to sit down. "You guys stay here, you wanted to drink. We'll see you later okay?"

"Uh, okay?" I raise my eyebrows. "But—"

"Yeah, you two have fun." Amanda nods three times.

"Are you sure?" Alex asks.

"Yeah, really. Have fun." Katherine slings her purse over her shoulder.

"Bye," they say in unison. They wave, turn around and disappear into the nearest street opening.

Alex glares. "Okay, what the fuck did we do?"

I shake my head. "I have no clue."

***

Kirsten knocks on the door at 12:13 a.m. I slink out of bed and let her in. I squint at the fluorescent light illuminating the hallway. Kirsten slides past me. I shut the door and lean against the closet. My tall shadow stretches out on the cold linoleum floor.

"How was the gelato?" I ask.

Kirsten unlatches her watch and places it on her nightstand. "Mm, delicious. We went to this place a few blocks from the Campo. Expensive, but so worth it. I got strawberry and chocolate, my favourite."

"Mmm." I fold my arms. "Sounds good. Did you come home with Evelyn by any chance?"

"Oh, no. She hung out with Pat and Andrew for the rest of night. God knows why." Kirsten scowls as she changes into her purple pyjama shorts and matching tank top. She hates Pat's loud and obnoxious manner. "They were playing drinking games before we left. Evelyn drank quite a bit."

"What?" I stand up straight. "She did?"

She's only ever had a few drinks in front of me.

"Mmm hmm." Kirsten pulls the covers over her chest. "Can you get the light?"

"Uh yeah, sure." I hit the switch and clamber into bed. I turn onto my side and stare out the window, past the green shudders, at the dark tree leaves illuminated by moonlight.

What could Evelyn possibly be mad at me about? I haven't done a thing. Not a goddamn thing.

I toss and I turn and I mull over the possibilities. Only one comes to mind.

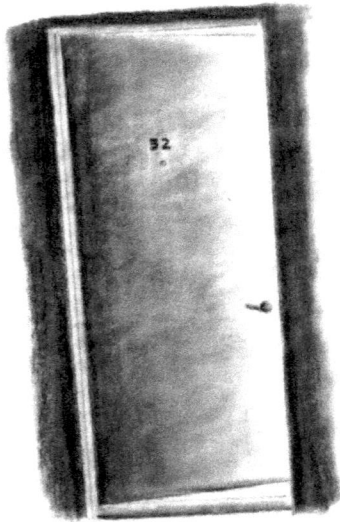

Chapter 15: Room 32

The door of Room 32 is ajar. I peek through the gap. Evelyn sprawls on the bed in her favourite outfit—a white undershirt and knee-length flannel pyjama pants—reading A Farewell to Arms. I shut my eyes and lightly rap my knuckles on the wood.

"Yes?"

I push the door open. Shards of light escape through partially opened blinds. The room is dim, even though it's 2 p.m. Books scatter on the desk, a towel hangs on a chair and shoes pile in the corner. The air is humid.

"Hi."

Evelyn's lips form a flat line. "Hey."

My chest tightens. "Are you busy?"

"Um." Evelyn's voice quavers. She looks around the mattress. "No, I guess not."

I press my hand on the door. "Can I come in?"

Evelyn sits upright and crosses her legs. She tosses her book and pen in front of her. She waits.

I tread into the room, leaving the door half open. "So, is something wrong? You seem upset."

"Well." Evelyn shakes her head. She sets her eyes on the garbage bin beside me. "Yeah, I am fucking upset."

I flinch. "About what?"

"About what?" Evelyn's voice hardens. "I don't appreciate being treated like garbage," she yells. "I'm a human being you know. I'm not just here to be fucked. I have feelings. I can't beli—"

My eyes widen. "What? What're you talking about?" I turn and glance across the hall to see if anyone can hear us. I spot Suzanna and Martha chatting on a bed listening to MGMT through their open door.

"Like what the fuck, Mary?" Evelyn glares at me. Her eyes are loaded, just waiting for me to pull the trigger.

I freeze, my hand reaching for the doorknob. "Can I close the door?" I stammer.

"I thought we were past all this bullshit. I thought we were communicating. I thought things were good. I feel like such an idiot." Evelyn smacks her forehead. "Here I was thinking, 'Oh, Mary.'" Evelyn mocks in a giddy, high-pitched voice and flutters her eyelashes. "'She's so great.' Then I find out you and Alex have been off fucking guys all weekend!"

"What?" I stutter. "What the fuck are you talking about?" My eyes dart back and forth between the open door and Evelyn.

All I can think about is closing that goddamn door and how I kissed Leo's neck in Rome at that sleazy club called The Cave. I only did it because I knew it meant nothing and that comforted me.

Who the fuck told her all this? Me and Alex never talked about Evelyn in front of the guys.

"I wasn't fucking guys all weekend!" My cheeks flush. "What the hell are you talking about?"

Evelyn lets out a low chuckle. "Oh, that's great, Mary. You're honestly going to stand here and lie to my face? Like do you have no fucking respect for me?" Evelyn's eyes glisten, but she does not break her gaze. "You think I'm insecure? That I'm just here to fucking entertain you or something?!"

I grit my teeth. I slide the garbage can out of the way and shut the door. The lock clicks. I sit down on the edge of the mattress, leaving Evelyn a foot of space. "What's going on? Where are you getting all this from?"

Evelyn clutches the piled sheets on the mattress. Her knuckles turn white. "I don't even know who the fuck you are anymore. I was bawling my eyes out all weekend, thinking how could this be true? I just couldn't believe what I was hearing." Her eyes drop to the floor and she shakes her head. "No way could it be Mary. No way did she say all those things."

"Evelyn!" I snap. "Tell me what's going on. I don't know what you're talking about! I get back from Rome and everyone is acting all weird. Katherine's ignoring me. You won't even look at me. What the fuck happened?"

Evelyn sneers.

"Evelyn," I growl. "Tell me what the fuck is going on!"

Our eyes lock.

"You honestly don't know?"

"No!" I shout.

Evelyn sighs. "Do you know why Katherine didn't come with you and Alex to Rome?"

"Katherine?" My eyes narrow. "Um, as far as I know… yeah. She was upset about her Dad's visit and she needed some time alone. And she had to study for her exam tomorrow."

"That's honestly what you think?"

"Um, yeah." I glare. "That's what she told me. What did she tell you?"

"Okay." Evelyn tucks her black bangs behind her ears. "The reason Katherine didn't come to Rome wasn't because of her Dad…"

My stomach fills with lead. Evelyn draws her words out slowly, like poison from a wound.

"…it was because of what you and Alex were saying the night before you left."

I clench my fists. I slowly nod and turn aside, careful not to let my emotions paint a picture on my face. I focus on the darkened dirt etched into the polyfill between the floor tiles.

The room blurs. I shut my eyes.

Fuck.

Anytime I had doubts about Evelyn, I went to Katherine. Every time I needed advice, I went to Katherine. Every moment Evelyn and I shared, I shared with Katherine. She's the one person who knows exactly how I feel about Evelyn. She's the one person I trusted without a doubt.

I open my eyes and turn to face Evelyn head on. "Okay. What did she say exactly?"

"Everything you and Alex were saying about us." Evelyn ticks the imaginary list off each of her fingers, her eyes ablaze. "How I'm insecure. How you decided you were gonna' fuck me and use me for sex. How you were pissed off when I started being affectionate with you because I was finally comfortable with it?" Her voice catches.

I lower my head and press my fingers into my temples. "Evelyn, that's not exactly—"

"Katherine's been ignoring you because she feels like she betrayed you. But she didn't want me getting hurt cause she thinks no one should be used like that."

"But—" I reach out to her.

Evelyn pulls back. "I told her she did the right thing. She said you scared the shit out of her on Friday and you weren't acting like yourself. And then you invited me back to your room after?" Evelyn shudders.

I pull my leg back, so as not to touch her. I can feel the cold, steel wall forming around her body. "What do you mean I wasn't acting like myself?"

"You weren't. We all noticed it. You were so angry and you wouldn't tell us what was wrong, even though I kept asking you. And when you invited me back to your room, you felt really off." Evelyn rubs her palms along her arms and legs, as if trying to wipe away the memory. Her eyes bore into the white wall. "You were being so aggressive."

I cringe, remembering how I forced myself upon her like I used to with guys, devoid of all emotion. "Okay, listen." I lean forward. "I was just in a really bad mood. And yeah, I did say those things. But I

81

didn't mean them. I was just running my mouth cause it felt good. I was never going to…" My voice cracks.

Evelyn's eyes bear down on me. "Going to what?"

I groan. "Fuck you. I wouldn't do that. I wouldn't have gone through with it. Alex kept saying all these things about how you were using me and I was just so exhausted and grumpy from Venice…" I exhale. "It seemed like a good idea at the time."

"Okay, you have to tell me what happened in Venice, Mary." Evelyn lowers her voice. "You were so angry."

I dig my fists into the mattress.

You're what made me so angry. I couldn't stop thinking about you.

"Nothing happened," I mutter. "I just hate travelling with Maria and them. I don't feel like I'm really friends with anyone in my class. I went just because it was Venice. We got lost the night we arrived and Maria and Natasha were just trying to pick up guys all weekend. I was exhausted and I just wanted to be here, with you guys."

"Really?" Evelyn frowns. "I thought you got along with the people in your class? I thought you were friends with Maria and that other chick."

I shrug. "I wouldn't call them friends. And the people in my class are fine. It's just different with you guys."

Evelyn chews her lip. "I didn't know that."

"Yeah, and I got back here and I really wanted to see you, but I was upset…" I steel myself. "Because you said you only wanted a fling."

Evelyn nods. "Okay, that's understandable. But, how could you say all those things? And then you invite me back to your room like that? You were being so aggressive. Your body felt so…" Her eyes search my face. "…hard." The word drops off her tongue like a dead weight. "You're normally so tender." Her voice softens. "Something wasn't right. I just thought you were upset, but…."

"I know, I know." I shake my head. My eyes trail across the details of the familiar black ink covering her feet. I recall brushing my fingers along the tattoo three short weeks ago.

"I wasn't going to do anything. I was upset with you, but once I held you again and we started talking…" My voice shakes. "I was never going to use you for sex, Evelyn. I was angry and I did say those things, but I could never do that to you. I see you as more than that." I look into her eyes. "I just wanted to detach myself. I didn't want to get hurt."

Evelyn groans. "This is just too fucked up. I don't know what you and Alex were doing all weekend, who you were fucking." She casts her eyes onto the floor. "I can't believe I almost slept with you."

"Evelyn..." I choke. I slide my hands over hers. "We got drunk one night. Nothing happened. I swear."

Evelyn pulls her hand back. "How am I supposed to trust you now? I can't believe you said all those things. It hurts to look at you."

"Evelyn... I..." My throat constricts.

I knew I should have stayed here. Fuck. But, I was just so angry. I can't believe I did this to her.

"Evelyn..." I rake my hands through my hair. "I didn't mean any of those things and I don't see you as an object. I really care about you. I never meant to hurt you." I lean forward. I want to hold her. I want to kiss her. But I can't.

"I don't know, Mary," Evelyn whispers. "How am I supposed to trust you again?"

"Evelyn." I pull her chin up. "Look at me."

Her naked, dark brown eyes find mine. They soften, slowly, and I fall, wholly consumed by her. "Do you believe what I'm saying to you right now?" I beg.

Evelyn falls quiet. Her eyes search my face. "I want to believe you. You seem sincere. You seem like the person I know."

I hold her gaze. "This is me. I'm here. I'm sorry."

I...

Laughter echoes in the room next door. Evelyn lets go of her grip on the sheets and falls back against the wall. I sink into the mattress, exhausted. "I'm really sorry, Evelyn. I care about you. A lot."

Evelyn nods. I stop myself from hugging her. A breeze of warm air hits our bodies. The laughter outside grows louder.

"So, are you done with me?" I whisper.

Evelyn blinks. "What? No. Of course not." She shakes her head. "You seem like you're telling the truth. And I know Alex played a big part in this. I don't blame you entirely."

I pull back. "Alex? What does she have to do with this?"

"Katherine was telling me that Alex kept pushing you and you were really upset and she kept filling your head with all this crap and turning you against me. Who does that to her so-called friends?"

"Wait, you think this is Alex's fault? She was just trying to help."

"Look Mary, I know she's your friend, but she's been using you. She never liked us together. She took you away to Rome for god's sake. You know this isn't just about sex and that's what she's been telling you."

"What?"

Alex did tell me to use Evelyn for sex, but she was just trying to protect me.

My mind drifts back to that night at the park. The night I brought Evelyn back to my room. I peer at Evelyn. She watches me intently.

Evelyn did say she wanted more than just sex. But, why would Alex push me away from her? Is she jealous?

A familiar throbbing strikes my temples and I am in the park again. Alex runs her mouth about Evelyn. Katherine watches nervously. Anger courses through my veins.

She did steal our bed in Cinque Terre. She even tried to cancel our date night. She pressured me to go to Rome. None of this would have happened if I had stayed.

I glance at Evelyn out of the corner of my eye. She jiggles her Monroe piercing back and forth, her gaze unrelenting.

She never liked Evelyn did she? Is Alex the one I should be watching?

My heart palpitates, anxiety setting in.

Whenever I'm with Evelyn, things are good. We talk things out. We're honest. Alex always makes me doubt Evelyn. Makes me doubt us.

Thoughts collide in my head. I turn aside from Evelyn.

Has she been manipulating me? How could she? She knows how I feel about Evelyn.

I stare at the black paint peeling off the leg of the desk chair. Rust seeps down the metal frame. "Mary?" Evelyn grabs my leg. I jump. "I know you two are good friends and you trusted her, but she's a bad person. She's been fooling all of us."

Look at the damage she's caused. I'll never be able to take back what I said.

I exhale slowly.

I trusted the wrong girl.

Evelyn wraps her eyes around me. "Look at all the problems she's caused between us. Between all of us. I mean, you're not even talking to Katherine now, Mary." I nod. "Katherine's been feeling so guilty about all this. She never meant to break your trust, Mary. But she was so overwhelmed and didn't know how far Alex had gotten into your head."

Evelyn squats cross-legged on the mattress. She's closer now. Within reach. "You're right." I whisper. "I can't believe I trusted her."

"So, what are you gonna' do?"

I sigh, my chest heaving. "Stop talking to her, I guess. If I can't trust her, how can I be friends with her?"

"And Katherine?"

"I'll talk to Katherine. I understand why she came to you. It's probably for the best. It's good to get these things out in the open."

Evelyn smiles. "I know it's hard. But, it's for the best, Mary."

"Yeah, I just can't believe I trusted her. She was my best friend."

A loud knocking strikes the door. Evelyn jumps. She crawls off the bed and opens the door. "Hey John!" she yelps.

"Hey Evelyn." John pops his head through the doorway. His unbuttoned plaid shirt hangs over his khaki shorts. "Oh. Hey Mary. Am I interrupting something?"

"No," Evelyn says quickly. "We're done. What's up?"

John slinks back into the hallway. His voice muffles. "I came by to see if you're still up for that art gallery?

"Oh, yeah! For sure." Evelyn turns around for a moment. "Just let me get dressed. I'll be right out." She closes the door.

"Art gallery?"

Evelyn rummages through her drawers. "Yeah. It's this gallery in town with modern canvases and stuff. I really want to check it out."

"Oh, okay." I stand up.

Evelyn slips into a white jean skirt and a red T-shirt with black stripes. She pulls her gladiator sandals from underneath the bed. I clasp her arm. "Are we good then?"

"Yeah, of course." Evelyn smiles.

I take her in my arms and I hug her. She loosely wraps her arms around my back. I close my eyes and squeeze her before letting go. Evelyn pecks me on the lips. I walk her out. John waits in the hallway outside. "I'm really sorry if I interrupted something."

Evelyn locks the door.

"It's fine." I smile. "Don't worry."

"Are you coming with us?" John asks.

I glance at Evelyn. She plays with her keychain.

"Um, no. I don't think so. I should really study for my exam tomorrow."

"Bummer. Alright, well if you change your mind it's just up on Rialto." John smiles. He strolls down the hallway with Evelyn close beside him.

I watch them walk away.

Chapter 16: A Resolution of Sorts

Alex and I face each other on the cobblestone street outside of Matteoli. Alex folds her arms across the chest of her yellow and brown leopard print dress. Lights from yellow and blue octopus shaped lanterns dance on the darkening street. The evening is wearing out.

She deserves an explanation, even if no one else thinks she does.

I agreed to speak with Alex after she approached us an hour ago, in the common room. Evelyn, Amanda, Katherine and I were laughing at Family Guy playing on the flat screen TV, munching on Archer Farm potato chips and sipping orange Fanta soda. Relief washed over me after I had patched things up with both Katherine and Amanda earlier on. They had discussed the matter at length over the weekend and agreed that Alex was being a mean girl, putting in her two cents about everyone's business far too often, to the detriment of our happiness. Even my roommate, Kristina, didn't care for Alex, but hadn't vocalized it earlier due to my friendship with her. Everything clicked. Alex is to blame for the issues within our group. Alex is the one who convinced me to go to Rome. Alex is trying to crush my romance with Evelyn. Alex has to go.

"What do you mean I was manipulating all of you?" Alex snaps. She places one hand on her hips and clutches her room key with the other.

"Okay, maybe not manipulating." I shrink back. "They were just saying that you've been shit talking a lot and they feel like they can't trust you. Us. After everything we said."

"Okay, but—"

"I apologized for everything." I interrupt. "Especially to Evelyn. I really hurt her." My eyes disappear up the street, to the park over-looking Siena. The park where I almost lost it.

If I hadn't said anything that night, none of this would have happened.

"Mary…"

I dig my heels into the ground.

"Look Alex, I'm not saying you had some big evil plan to fuck with all of our heads but you were giving me a lot of bad advice about Evelyn. Telling me to use her was wrong. She doesn't deserve that." I envision Evelyn crying in her room while Alex and I were plastered in Rome. "She doesn't deserve that."

Alex uncrosses her arms. "I wasn't trying to give you bad advice. I was trying to help you." She opens her hands toward me. I freeze. "When a friend is upset over a guy or a girl or whoever, you say he's a jerk and you talk smack about him. I was just trying to be there for you. It really wasn't my plan to cause problems between you and Evelyn." Alex's voice falters, the edge to her character fading.

I swallow hard and set my shoulders straight. Evelyn warned me not to let Alex soften me, manipulate me. "Yeah, but you did."

Voices echo inside the corridor of Matteoli. I peer inside. Nicole and Jen skip past the arched entrance holding bottles of Pinot Noir. "Hey, guys!" Nicole smiles. "How's it going?"

Alex mutters under her breath. "Uh, good." I feign a smile.

"Oh." Nicole glances at Alex. "Sorry. We didn't mean to inter-rupt anything."

Jen's eyes widen. Nicole nudges her. They smile tightly. "We were just heading out."

"Yeah, yeah we were," Jen sputters. "To the piazza."

"Sorry to interrupt, we'll catch you later." Nicole grabs Jen's arm and leads her up the street. They step into a glowing pizzeria a few blocks up.

I turn to Alex. She paces the street, her hand pressed to her forehead. The sun sinks lower and the street darkens. The lanterns cast cruel shadows on Alex, their twisting octopus tentacles reaching for her like prey. The air is thick with humidity, but I can feel the cool of autumn settling in.

I shake my head.

This wasn't supposed to end this way.

A knot twists in my stomach and climbs up my throat. I swallow it.

You're doing the right thing. Evelyn is right… She has to be.

"Look." I jam my clammy hands into my green khaki shorts' pockets. "I'm not blaming you, because I took your advice and I'm responsible for my actions, but…" I shut my eyes and steady myself for the blow I am about to deliver. Evelyn's words spill from my lips. "I feel like you're a bad person. I don't know if I can trust you now."

Alex's face contorts.

"What has Evelyn been saying to you?" her voice cracks.

My chest tightens. "Don't get Evelyn involved." I snarl. "That's not what this is about."

Alex scoffs. "Of course that's what this is about! She's manipulating you. Can't you see that?" Alex reaches forward.

I hold my arms in front of me. "Don't Alex."

"Mary." Alex pleads. "Look at me."

I run my hands through my hair and feel beads of sweat on my forehead. I look up at Alex. Her eyes glisten. "Do you honestly believe everything they're saying?" Alex's voice trembles. "I never meant to hurt anyone. I consider you a really good friend. I don't want to lose your friendship this way." Alex grasps my arm. "You have to believe what I'm saying to you." I take another step back. Alex's watery eyes bear down on me. Evelyn's deep, seductive voice whispers in my ear.

***

"Mary, she's going to tell you not to believe me. She's going to try and take you away from us." Evelyn had tucked my bangs behind my ears. "Don't let her."

"I won't."

I kissed her again for the first time since our fight. She kissed me back.

***

"Alex, I just..." I somehow manage to look right at her. "I just can't trust you after everything you've said. This is too much. I can't deal with all of this." My stomach lurches. "The trip is over in a few days. I just want to go home."

"Mary, I consider you a really good friend. Please don't do this." Tears stream down her face. My heart wrenches. I run through the last few days in my mind, searching for another answer, for another way. But, Evelyn is my only answer. I have been waiting years to feel this way. I cannot let her go.

I back away. "I'm sorry, Alex. I really am. But, I just can't trust you. Not after what I did to Evelyn."

"So, that's it?" Alex pushes her glasses onto her head and rubs the tears away.

The knot in my stomach tightens. "Yeah, that's it."

***

The rolling hills of Tuscany whirr past the window of the bus from Florence to Siena. Evelyn sits beside me, her large black headphones wrapped around her neck and her tattooed feet perched on the rubber railing in front of us.

"So..." I sink into the green cushioned chair. "Are you sure you're okay?"

Evelyn glimpses at me through her cat's eye sunglasses. "Yeah, I told you. We all fuck up. You're only human. I know I have before. It's in the past." She shrugs. "Honestly."

"Yeah, but that doesn't make it okay..."

"Your apology was all that I needed to move on. Alex manipulated all of us. You thought she was your friend and you trusted her. It's okay."

I nod. A vineyard filled with rows of leafy vines and narrow dirt lanes blurs as we drive past. "It's just..." I rub my sweating legs. "I feel so bad. I mean, you said it hurt for you to look at me. It was really hard for me to hear that."

"Aw, Mary." Evelyn drops her legs to the floor and turns to face me. "Don't beat yourself up about this. I know you were just letting off steam when you said those things. I won't judge you for it."

"Are you sure?"

"I'm sure."

"Okay." I slide my fingers into Evelyn's hand. She smiles, lifts my hand up to her mouth and kisses it. We hold hands and press close to each other as the miles fly by. Passengers snooze, listen to music or chat with each other in the rows spreading out before us. Amanda and Katherine sit behind us, showing each other the leather purses and suitcases they purchased in the leather market in Florence.

I squeeze Evelyn's hand. "Yes?"

I take a deep breath.

Ask her.

"Do you want to keep this going when we get back to Toronto?"

Evelyn falters. Her mouth draws open. "Uh—"

"We can keep things casual." I blurt. "Keep getting to know each other and see how it goes?" I watch her closely.

"Yeah." Evelyn nods. "I totally agree. I definitely want to keep seeing you... Sonya's not gonna' be happy about it though." My gut clenches. I had forgotten about Sonya. "She gets really jealous, but I don't care. I'm just gonna' have to tell her about you."

"She's not gonna' come after me and try to beat me up is she?" I chuckle nervously.

Evelyn shakes her head. "No, no. I wouldn't let her do that. But, she is very possessive. Like even at bars, she literally blocks other girls off with her arms." Evelyn told me Sonya is six feet tall with a thick build. I'm five foot six with a lean frame.

Jesus. She could kick my ass.

"And in bed, she's well..."

I grip the armrests of my seat.

"It was..." Evelyn scrunches her nose.

Oh my god. Why is she telling me this?

"She's a lot bigger than me so..."

I lock my eyes on the other passengers. I focus on an old woman reading a newspaper.

Please stop talking, please stop talking.

"Um, maybe you don't want to hear about this."

Oh, thank god.

My muscles relax. "No, not really. You can stop there."

"Never mind Sonya. I wanna' enjoy my Mary time." Evelyn snuggles her head against my shoulder and tightens her grip around my hand. I lean my head on hers and close my eyes.

The scent of lavender and vanilla and the music streaming from Evelyn's headphones lull me into a deep, blissful sleep.

Chapter 17: Toronto

We arrive at Pearson Airport on a warm Saturday afternoon on September 5, 2009. Evelyn lays affectionate kisses and flirtatious remarks on me. She talks about how she'll have me over at her apartment in the Annex. I want to smell the lavender incense she lights in her living room where she reads novels in the evening. I want to see her white painted room with bright turquoise tables and dressers, and the chocolate brown bookshelf her grandfather made for her. I want to run my hands along her queen size bed with a thick, black duvet and dozens of yellow and red pillows. But most of all, I want to jump into her bed and hear her soft moaning in my ears and taste her wet thighs and press my tongue into her with the rhythm of her breathing. Just the way she had said to do during that night out at the Barone Rosso. I hope to get what I wasn't ready for when I met her.

Evelyn and I joke about how awkward it will be if our parents arrive at the same time to pick us up. How we won't be able to press our lips together and squeeze each other goodbye.

I pull my luggage behind me, past Arrivals and into the crowded

Terminal C. I want to kiss Evelyn goodbye. But, when I turn around, she isn't there. I shrug it off. We don't need the clichéd parting kiss. We both live in the GTA. This isn't your typical vacation fling. We have plans to keep seeing each other.

***

Thursday is the only day of the week that Dad goes to the office, normally working out of his spacious den on the main floor at home. I should be sitting on a plastic orange bucket chair in a cramped classroom in the North Building at the University of Toronto, Mississauga. Syllabi with a course description, a list of readings, due dates and a severe warning about academic plagiarism for HIS 395 - The Renaissance, are being passed around the classroom.

It's been a week and three days since we landed in Toronto. Evelyn has only responded to one of the three messages I left for her on Facebook. I apologized for not kissing her goodbye. She told me I was cute and that I owed her a kiss when we saw each other next. I drove all the way to the Danforth in Toronto last Sunday to see her during a shisha session at the Hot Pot Café. Anthony came. Katherine came. Amanda came. Even Kirsten and her boyfriend Mario came. Evelyn did not text, call or Facebook message me the next day about not showing up.

I refuse to contact her.

I always make the effort. She can come to me this time.

I sink into the light brown sofa in our family room. I prop my feet up on the coffee table stained with water marks, a burn from our iron and chipping veneer. Smooth saxophone and deep bass stream out of the Sony stereo playing Jazz FM 91.1.

I hate weekday morning jazz. Dad puts that shit on every morning.

I walk over to the sunroom and hit the power button on the stereo. Jude, our yellow budgie with blue and green spots jumps onto the thin, metal bars of his cage, chirping and squawking.

"Oh, shut up!" I bark.

I plunk back down onto the sofa. I grab my LG Rumour cell phone off the table and scroll to Katherine's number. I purse my lips.

I shouldn't get her involved. What is she gonna' say anyways?

I tap the back button twice, lock the screen and toss the phone onto the couch. I sip my homemade espresso. It tastes bitter. I grumble and walk over to the kitchen and add more milk and sugar. I grimace. Too sweet.

"Fucking coffee tastes like shit here," I mutter.

I set the white porcelain cup down on the coffee table. It wobbles, echoing in our large, empty suburban house.

If you're not gonna' get in touch with Evelyn, you might as well call Katherine. Get some feedback. She knows both of you. She'll know what to do.

The phone rings three times.

"Hallo?" Katherine says in a high-pitched, German accent.

I chuckle. "Hey, what's up?"

"Oh, nothing really. I'm supposed to be in class, but I skipped. I'm still super jet-lagged. What about you?"

"Oh yeah? Wow, you're really sensitive eh?"

"Yes, you know this."

"Yeah. I'm supposed to be in class right now too. But, I dunno. I just didn't feel like going. This stuff with Evelyn's been really bugging me."

Katherine shouts to her Mom in Czech. I hear a fridge door slam. "Sorry about that. What's bugging you about Evelyn?"

"Um." I take a sip of espresso. "Well. She hasn't gotten back to me since like last Thursday and then she bailed on Sunday. I know you said she had a family thing that night, but still..." I pick up The Toronto Star and scan the GTA Section. "I don't know if I should call her or just leave it alone or— "

"I think you should just let it go. I mean if she hasn't contacted you..."

"Let it go?" my voice crackles through the receiver. I toss the newspaper onto the couch. "Why would you say that?"

Katherine softens her tone. "Mary, I just don't think she's as serious about it as you are. Look at you, you're already getting upset just 'cause she hasn't spoken to you in a while. You knew she didn't want a relationship."

I scoff. "Well yeah, but..." I pull myself up off the couch and walk into the hallway. My bare feet pound across the hardwood floors. Sunlight beams through the glass window of our front door. I shield my eyes. "I never said I wanted one either. I just wanted to give things a shot here. See how things went." Jude's squawks follow me up the carpeted staircase. I shut my bedroom door. The squawking fades. "She said the same thing." I turn on my 20" Panasonic TV and flip through the channels, stopping at Jerry Springer. A heavyset, balding man wearing a stained, white wife beater stands up and shouts at two cowering girls. The subtitle scrolls across the bottom of the screen. Today on Jerry Springer: FEMALE ADULTERERS, CRAZED EX-HUSBAND.

"Okay," Katherine says. "I didn't want to tell you this because I don't want to get involved and be the go between but— "

"Tell me what?" I lie down on my bed and stretch my neck up onto the body pillow. "If it's something about Evelyn, I think I deserve to know."

Katherine sighs. "Okay, but don't get upset."

I bury my feet underneath my white IKEA duvet. "I won't."

"I went out to dinner with Evelyn last Thursday."

I inhale through my clenched teeth.

She had time to see Katherine and she couldn't even call me?

"Okay…"

"She's been really busy with school and work and everything and…" Katherine pauses.

"Yes?" I sit upright.

"And she told Sonya about you."

I wrap the body pillow around me. "Oh. And?"

Steve the bodyguard wears a tight black T-shirt over his bulging muscles. He grabs the man by the shoulders and pulls him off the stage. "JERRY! JERRY!" the crowd chants.

"And…" Katherine groans. "Sonya got really jealous and she told Evelyn to stop seeing you."

I clutch the body pillow curled around my body. "JERRY! JERRY!" The man in the stained undershirt swings a punch at Steve but misses. "JERRY! JERRY!" the chanting grows. The crowd rises. The receiver crackles.

"Mary?"

"Yeah." I shake my head. "Sorry. Go ahead."

"She said that she would."

My chest heaves and sinks deep into the pit of my stomach. I stare at the TV screen. Steve pummels the man and drags him off stage. The crowd falls quiet. Jude's chirping slips underneath my closed door.

"Mary?"

My lip quivers.

"Look, it's for the best. Sonya and her did start seeing each other before you did. And Sonya is friends with her cousin and Evelyn hangs out with them a lot."

I spot a faint reflection of my slouching body on the TV screen. Steve tromps across my face. He returns to the stage, grinning and takes a bow.

My eyes water. "But, but I don't get it. She told me she wanted to keep seeing me... They had only been dating a few weeks."

"Mary... she just doesn't feel the same way as you do. You're going to get hurt. I can tell you're already hurt. Don't make it worse."

Tears stream down my face. "But..." I sputter.

"Mary," Katherine says sternly. "You have to let it go."

My arms tremble. I close my eyes. "How?"

"Try to be friends with her. She's an amazing girl. She'll understand if you need some time."

"Okay," I mumble. "If that's what she wants."

I fall back onto the pillow and close my eyes. I try to speak but my mouth is too dry.

"Mary, you'll get over it. Just give it time."

"Thanks, Katherine." I sputter. "I'll talk to you later." I drop my LG onto the carpeted floor.

I peer up at the glow-in-the-dark sticker stars peeling off the white stucco ceiling of my bedroom. Mom helped me tape them to the ceiling when I was eight years old. It made me feel safe in the dark.

"Steve! Steve! Steve!" the crowd roars.

I crawl underneath the covers. I soak my body pillow in tears and hug the soft stuffing. I shut my eyes, stifle my sobs and give in to the darkness.

There's no place like home.

Chapter 18: Wake-up Call

Sunlight peeps through the bamboo blinds hung across the window and cascades down the red walls of Ms. Nemec's bedroom. Katherine's mom is spending the weekend at her boyfriend's cottage. Her master bedroom acts as a guest room for me, outfitted with red oak hardwood flooring and a separate bathroom with Jacuzzi and shower. I spent the night here after going out for shisha at the Hot Pot Café with Katherine, her friend Abia and my close friend Lesia. I wanted to take my mind off Evelyn and escape my parents' house for the weekend.

My Roots backpack slouches against the white armchair in the corner of the room and my jeans, black hoodie and brown TNA jacket clutter the floor. My body sinks into the firm yet soft bed in the centre of the room. The sheets caress my warm skin and the duvet hugs me better than any girl ever could.

Beeeeep.

My eyes snap open. My cell phone rings in my ear. I grumble and pull my arms from underneath the cocoon of soft sheets and white feather duvet. I squint at the blurry, glowing red numbers on the black Panasonic alarm clock.

8:36 am! Who the fuck is texting me? This better be important.

I throw my arm on the nightstand and fumble for my LG Rumour. The screen lights up.

Text Message Received

Fr: Evelyn

My head jerks back and slams the headboard.

"Fuck," I mumble and rub the back of my head. I kick the tangle of duvet and sheets off and push the soft pillows up against the headboard. I clutch my phone. Evelyn has never contacted me by phone. My eyes trip over the text message.

I had a dream last night that we were watching A&E together. We were holding hands and I was caressing yours. You looked at me like I was crazy hehe. It was nice seeing you though, even if it was only in my dreams.

The corners of my mouth arch upwards into a wide grin. I read the text again.

It was nice seeing you though, even if it was only in my dreams.

I bite my lip and twirl on the hardwood floor, hugging my phone. I read it again.

I had a dream last night...

Wait.

I shut my eyes.

No. Fuck. Stop it! You're trying to be friends!

I read the text again. I groan.

Fuck, fuck, fuck, fuuuuuuck!

I chuck my LG Rumour into the messy pile of sheets. I stomp to the bathroom. I drop my red satin pajamas pants to the floor and sit on the toilet. I stare at the New Yorker magazines littering the counter, the Dove shampoo bottles lining the shower shelf and the gleaming silver faucet.

Fucker. Why did she send me that text? I was finally okay with things.

I flush the toilet. The water sloshes in circles around the bottom of the bowl and is sucked down the drain. I wash my hands with soap and cold water.

Don't do it. Don't text her back. You'll relapse.

I stare at my sunken hazelnut eyes, untamed eyebrows and disheveled brown hair in the mirror.

God, you look like shit.

I shut the bathroom door and climb back into bed with my LG Rumour. I pull the covers up to my shoulders. I purse my lips.

Just don't be flirty.

My fingers dance across the qwerty keyboard.

What happened next?

I bury my head in the pillow.

Delete.

Tap tap tap. Tap tap tap.

Is that all we were doing?

"Ugh." I push the blankets to the edge of the bed and sit cross-legged on the bare mattress.

Delete.

I take a deep breath.

Don't give in. Just be friendly.

I type slowly.

Right on, she can't read anything into that.

Text Message Sent

Fr: Mary

Wakey wakey early on a Sunday morning eh? What's A&E?

I slide across the mattress and hug the pile of pillows and sheets. The neighbour's Jack Russell Terrier's barks echo through St. Claire Avenue West.

Beeeeep.

Text Message Received

Fr: Evelyn

Yeah :) I didn't go out last night. I went to bed early. Yeah, the channel…

I stare at the screen. I type out a response three different ways.

Don't give her what she wants. Don't confirm it.

I want to know that she's still into me. I want to know that we have something, anything, even if it's just flirting. I cringe and glance away as the envelope flies across the screen.

Text Message Sent

Fr: Mary

Oh, okay. I thought so. As much as I hate being woken up, I'll let it slide since it is nice waking up to a text from you.

I hop out of bed and peer out the window at Katherine's gazebo in the backyard. Fallen leaves scatter on the grass. They skip and jump at the wind's beckoning, twirling dirt and debris into a frenzy.

Beeeep.

Text Message Received

Fr: Evelyn

Hehehehe

"Ugh." I bang my fist on the window.

Fucking idiot. She has you now.

The faint reflection of my face shakes its head at me in the window. I close the blinds. I switch my LG to Silent Mode and drop it on the nightstand. It hits the clock radio and skids to the edge. I bury myself in sheets, pillows and duvet and whack my face into the mattress.

Perfect morning, just perfect.

***

Chuchi, Katherine's black Tibetan Terrier, scampers across the hallway and into the kitchen, barking. Her paws scratch the hardwood floor as she runs toward me. "Chuchi!" I shout in a baby voice and take a seat on the black leather sofa near the patio door. "Come here." Chuchi's tongue hangs out and she jumps up my leg. I grab her by the scruff and rub her head, neck and ears. "Aw, you're so cute, Chuchi."

Katherine shakes her head and laughs. "You really need a dog, Mary."

"Yesh, I know. Don't I, Chuchi?" I grin and rub my hand over her belly.

"Do you take cinnamon in your coffee?" Katherine holds a bag of President's Choice African Roast.

"You put cinnamon in your coffee?" I push Chuchi off my leg and walk over to the black marble counter separating the kitchen and living room. I rub the dog hairs clinging to my hand onto my black Batman T-shirt.

"Uh, yeah." Katherine laughs. "You've never heard of that before?"

"Nope." I shake my head. "Go for it. It sounds good."

I pull two Eggo waffles out of the yellow cardboard box. "Mmm. I haven't had Eggos since we got back." I drop the frozen waffles into the toaster and press the lever down.

"Eat all you want." Katherine shuts the lid to the Hamilton Beach coffee machine and flicks the switch on.

"Thanks." I grab my LG Rumour from the counter and fiddle with the buttons. "So, don't freak out or anything." I take a deep breath. "But, I have something to show you."

Katherine raises her eyebrows. I scroll down to Evelyn's text message and hold out the phone. She gasps. "Evelyn sent this to you!" I nod.

"When?"

"This morning at like eight-thirty. I had to wake up to that shit." The coffee machine chortles and hisses. A thin stream of hot, black coffee splashes into the bottom of the clear coffee pot. "It gets worse. Wait till you see my response." I pull up my sent messages and hand the LG back.

Katherine groans. "Oh, no, Mary. Please tell me you did not send that."

"Oh, I did." I run my hands through my hair. I pace the hardwood floors, my bare feet thudding on the wood. "I know, I know. I shouldn't have. But I couldn't resist. She was being so flirty!"

Katherine shakes her head. "This is not cool. She shouldn't have sent that."

"Yeah, no shit. She's playing games with me." My Eggos pop out the toaster. I toss the hot waffles onto my plate and dribble syrup over them. "This woman is going to be the death of me!"

Katherine bends over to pet Chuchi. She gazes out of the patio door with a spotted navy blue coffee cup in her hands. "This really isn't right. She has Sonya. I don't understand why she's continuing this."

"Because." I cut into the crispy, golden waffles. "She wants to know she can still have me." I stab my fork into a piece dripping in syrup. "And I gave her that."

"Fuck," Katherine mutters. "So are you coming tonight?"

"I don't know." I stare at my cell phone. "We'll see."

Chapter 19: Shisha Darkness

Thick streams of translucent smoke cling to the fading orange walls of the Hot Pot Café on Danforth Avenue. Dim lamps, covered with dirt stains and yellow watermarks, hang from the ceiling. Patrons chatting in Arabic pack the cafe in groups of seven to eight. They sit on thick, embroidered cushions and lean on long, colourful pillows, playing dominos and eating roast chicken, beef kebabs and fool ma`rizz rice with raisins. They smoke shisha from large hookahs at their feet and greet friends who have just stepped in from the chilly September air. Today is Eid-el-Fitr, the celebratory feast after Ramadan.

Amanda and I sit at a wooden table across from a glass counter filled with soda, water and cookies. A tiny metal bell hanging off the glass door chimes. Katherine holds the door open for Evelyn and Anthony. I slouch into my chair and grip the seat. This is my first glimpse of Evelyn since our arrival at Pearson Airport. The door slams shut.

"Hey everyone!" Evelyn grins, her cheeks rosy. Anthony waves and shrugs off his denim jacket. Evelyn wears tight black skinny jeans that tuck into her purple suede Vans sneakers. Her dark hair is pulled back into a high ponytail and dark mascara and eyeliner mask her eyes. She runs over and hugs me from behind. My shoulders twitch. I pat her arms. Katherine pulls out the chair beside me and takes a seat. Anthony grabs the seat beside Amanda. Evelyn slips into the one across from me.

My body trembles. I force a smile.

Evelyn folds her arms over the table and leans forward. "So, what's new, everybody? It's been what, like two weeks? I'm assuming something has happened." She laughs. I run my eyes over Evelyn.

She looks so different. Why is she wearing all that make-up?

"Well, I just got a job at the Media Commons in Robarts." Amanda answers first. "I'm really excited about it. I get to watch movies all day."

"Oh, that's awesome! I'm so happy for you. I actually just quit my job at Fly nightclub." Evelyn rolls her eyes. "Finally." Her voice is jittery. She clasps her hands on the table, a smile plastered to her face. I slouch further into my chair.

"Well I already talked to you." Katherine pokes at the silver lip ring she had done a few days ago. "I'm sure you don't need to hear it again."

Evelyn nods. "How about you, Anthony?"

"I've been good." Anthony rolls up the sleeves of his blue flannel shirt. "I've been busy all week. But I'm all moved into my new place on campus and my courses are going pretty well." He pushes his glasses onto the bridge of his nose and glances at me.

Evelyn nods her head. Up and down. Up and down. She turns to me. "What about you, Mary?"

My hands tremble underneath the table. "I'm good." My voice shakes. I sit up and tuck my hands into the pockets of my black zip-up hoodie. "Classes are alright. I made it onto the football team." I rub the back of my neck. "Well... everyone who tried out made it." I laugh. "Oh, and I caught the ball during the tryout... so that's good."

My eyes widen.

You caught the ball? Seriously?

I catch Anthony smirking out of the corner of my eye. I jam my fists back into my hoodie. "Cool." Evelyn smiles politely. Amanda and Anthony nod. Abia stands up to greet a friend at the door. Katherine toys with her lip ring. Evelyn's eyes dart around the café buzzing with conversation. She tucks a stray hair behind her ear and folds her hands on the table. She smiles for the third time. "Oh my gosh! I almost forgot!" She pulls back the sleeves of her beige windbreaker. "Look at this!" A red rash climbs from her wrist to her elbow.

"Oh my god!" Anthony holds his hand over his mouth.

"That's so gross." Katherine grimaces. "Ew."

Evelyn displays her arm on the table like an artifact. "Turns out I did get stung by a jellyfish at Ossessione beach. Me and Sonya thought it was bed bugs, so we stripped the entire bed. We were freaking out." I envision Evelyn and Sonya jumping out of bed half-naked, shrieking and giggling. I stare at a chunk of hard gum plastered to the floor. "So I'm on prescription pills right now to get rid of the infection. It spread to my entire body."

Oh god.

I clamp my mouth shut.

Anthony leans back in his chair and raises his eyebrows at me behind Amanda's head. His lips move as he tries to mouth something. He nudges his head towards Evelyn. I roll my eyes. I haven't told him about my chat with Katherine yet. I slump into my chair. I check the time on my LG Rumour. 9:14 p.m.

***

I grasp my knees to steady my shaking legs. Evelyn sits beside me on the worn red sofa, with her legs crossed. Thin ribbons of smoke slither through the air. My head pounds and my eyes sting. I rub the contact lenses against my dry pupils.

There she is. You've been waiting this long to see her and now you can't even open your mouth. Why the fuck did you come here?

"Mary," Anthony whispers in my ear. "I think you should excuse yourself. You look really anxious."

Anthony and I have been leaning on each other for the last two weeks. Matthew keeps asking Anthony for more patience, to give him space and to hold out for him. He'll be ready for a relationship soon. I have nothing to hold out for. Anthony knows it. I know it. Everybody fucking knows it. "Are you serious? Oh my god. I'll be right back." I climb over Anthony, hop over the couch and head for the bathroom.

No way I'm climbing over her.

I pace the narrow hallway cluttered with cardboard boxes and milk cartons. Two giggling Arabic girls step out of the small, boxed bathroom. They edge their way past me. I step inside. My white Puma sneaker splashes into a small puddle on the ground.

Ew. I don't even want to know what that is.

I hop over the puddle and lock the door. I study my reflection in the greasy mirror. I breathe deeply.

In and out. In and out.

Get a grip, Mary. She's just a girl. You can do this.

I close my eyes and breathe in and out ten times. I brace my shoulders, swing the door open and march up the stairs. I sink into the cushions beside Evelyn. Anthony chats into my ear to distract me from her. Four inches separate our thighs. I want to keep it that way.

***

The green glass hookah sitting on the floor beside Anthony's thigh bubbles as he inhales. He smiles and passes me the hose. I finally start to relax after the moist, double apple shisha fills my lungs for the eighth time. I stretch my legs underneath the wooden table.

Anthony and I have been talking non-stop, as have Katherine and her two friends, Fatima and Abia. Amanda went home at midnight, to catch the last subway train. Evelyn eyes her purple suede Vans sneakers.

Say something. You've been ignoring her all night.

"So, Evelyn." I turn to face her. "Did you end up going to that LGBTQ Meet n' Greet?"

LGBTQ is the Lesbian, Gay, Bisexual, Transgendered and Queer student group at the University of Toronto. LGBTQ groups operate at most university and college campuses, offering resources such as counselling, information sessions and social events.

"Oh." Evelyn pivots on the couch. "Yeah, I did. It's not really what I'm looking for though. I think it's more for people trying to gain a connection to the gay community. I already have that, so I don't think I'll be going back."

"Oh… okay."

My stomach churns.

Of course you have that. You have Sonya.

"Hey, Mary." Anthony pokes me. "Is it cool if I get a ride home with you? I'm just off of St. George and Bloor."

"Yeah, sure. If it's on the way."

"Thanks, Mary."

I bite my lip. "Do you need a lift, Evelyn?"

Evelyn's eyes fall on me, wide as ever. "Oh, um." Her voice shakes. She clears her throat. "No. It's okay. I'll take a cab."

I lean back on the couch, my eyes on hers. "Are you sure? It's no problem, really."

I want to talk to her alone. See her alone. She must feel something for me.

Evelyn looks past me, at Anthony. "Well, if it's not too much trouble."

I smile. "It's totally fine. You're both on the way."

***

The lights from Margaret Addison Hall, Anthony's residence building, shine on the dashboard of my parent's four-door Saturn Ion. Metric's "Help I'm Alive" ripples through the speakers.

"I tremble. They're going to eat me alive. If I stumble. They're going to eat me alive."

I pull off to the side of the road. "Thank you so much, Mary." Anthony hugs me. He whispers into my ear. "We'll talk soon okay?"

I smile. "Thanks, Anthony. I'll call you later. Good night."

"Good night." Anthony steps out of the vehicle.

"Evelyn, do you wanna' hop into the front?"

"Oh, sorry." Anthony holds the passenger door open. "Yeah, you can come up front."

"Oh." Evelyn pauses. "Yeah, sure."

Evelyn shimmies into the front seat. The door slams shut. Anthony mouths something about being careful as Evelyn's seatbelt clicks. He crosses the street, reaches the glass doors and waves good-bye.

"Can you hear my heart beating like a hammer? / Beating like a hammer? / Help, I'm alive, my heart keeps beating like a hammer / Hard to be soft / Tough to be tender"

I shift the car into drive. "Where to?"

"Just keep driving straight."

I nod. The car rolls forward.

"So, what're you up to for the week?"

Evelyn rubs her fingernails, scratching at the black nail polish. "Not too much. I have to take care of some things at the registrar. They fucked up my anthro credit. I can't take the prerequisite 'til next term."

I slow down at the stop sign. "That sucks. Keep going straight?" I point ahead.

"Yeah, just keep driving past these intersections and then it's a left on Albany."

"'kay."

"Come take my pulse, the pace is on a runaway train / Help, I'm alive, my heart keeps beating like a hammer / Beating like a hammer."

I accelerate through the Annex neighbourhood. The red and yellow bulbs on the massive Honest Ed's sign flicker. Customers bring cups of coffee to their lips and dig forks into cheesecakes and brownies at Future Bakery. They laugh and smile with one another, some on dates, others with friends.

I grind my teeth.

Well aren't they having a lovely evening?

Evelyn's voice softens. "How have you been?" She glances at me with doe eyes. Mine feel like lead.

I grip the steering wheel and hook a left on Albany. "Good. Just getting back into the rhythm of things. It's rough living with my parents." I shrug. "But, whatever."

"It'll be a lot better once you move out. Just stick it out." Evelyn pulls out her keychain. "You can stop here."

I press my Puma sneaker onto the brake pedal. "This is fine?"

"Yeah."

"If you're still alive / My regrets are few / If my life is mine / What shouldn't I do?"

I turn down the volume. My heart pounds in rhythm with the speakers.

Evelyn turns in the seat. "So, it was really good to see you."

My throat closes. Evelyn opens her arms. I lean forward and hug her small frame. I pull back quickly. Evelyn lays her eyes on me. "Keep trekking out to the city to see us okay? Hopefully I'll see you soon?" I meet her gaze and sketch her face in my mind, knowing that I may never see her again.

My tongue numbs. I can think of nothing to say to keep her in this car with me.

"Yeah." I feign a smile.

"Good night." Evelyn hops out.

The passenger door bangs shut, rattling the car. I watch her cross the street and disappear into the shadow of the apartment building I so desperately wanted to be let into. I slam the accelerator and find my way back to Bloor and Spadina. My hands tremor on the steering wheel. I turn up the volume.

"I get wherever I'm going / I get whatever I need / While my blood's still flowing / And my heart still beats…."

I speed past the series of yellow street lights. College Street. Dundas Street West. Queen Street West. King Street West.

I pull onto the QEW West highway. The car speakers vibrate.

"Beating like a hammer / Beating like a hammer"

The yellow lines separating the lanes blur in and out of focus. I wipe my wet eyes with the sleeve of my black hoodie. I grip the steering wheel and stare at the asphalt road and the passing yellow lines.

Don't get in an accident, Mary. Don't get in an accident.

I exit at Erin Mills Parkway. I park the car. The garage door slams behind me. I hang the car key on the hook in the kitchen. The humming of the dishwasher fills the main floor. Shaking, I collapse onto the family room couch. Tears drench my face and my hands tremble. I muffle my sobs with a red satin pillow. A searing pain shoots through my temples. How the fuck could someone have this effect on me? How could sitting beside some girl almost give me an anxiety attack? Why does she have this hold over me?

I bury my wet face into the pillow, staining it a bloody crimson.

I cry until the pain fades and my tears dry and I'm too exhausted to do anything other than sleep.

Chapter 20: A Subway Farewell

I spent hours, days, weeks and eventually months, searching for a loop-hole in our relationship. A relationship only in my mind, not hers. What had been a life-altering experience for me was just a fling to her. She had a woman waiting for her, a solid lesbian identity in her back-pocket and a sweet-ass apartment in the Annex. I didn't want to think about finding another girl, coming out to my parents and getting a part-time job. Getting through the fall semester at the U of T's Mississauga campus was more than enough. One day I would feel jubilant, free and excited to be moving on, the next day I'd stare out into space and relive every moment of our intimacy as if it were some precious jewel not to be lost or forgotten.

Oh, and the crying. Oh, dear god, the crying—on the floor of my sunroom with jazz playing in the background, during the middle of a phone call with my older sister begging her for advice on how to make the pain go away, on my couch watching Bend It Like Beckham, mornings in bed when I didn't want to move. The sheer shock of the emotional experience left me stunned and reeling. All the guys

I had met, dated, fooled around with, wanted to have sex with—none of them had this effect of me. I thought I was immune to the insanity of romantic attachment. Turns out I'm just not straight.

***

My friend, Dave and I hop onto the TTC subway car at Dundas West Station at around 4 o'clock on a Thursday afternoon in early January. We had met up in the Roncesvalles neighbourhood to edit our stories and grab dinner.

I walk through the first car, grasping the metal railings. A black woman in her early thirties reads The Globe and Mail. She glances up at me and places her hand over the Prada purse beside her. I roll my eyes. The teenager across from her bobs his head and rolls his thumb along the volume of his blue iPod Nano. Newspapers, water bottles and chip wrappers clutter the faded burgundy seats as I pass by them. I stop at a three-seater bench facing sideways. I plunk down on the middle seat. Dave joins me. I drop my bag to the floor and unzip my coat. I look up at the girl in front of me. She's completely engrossed in a white paperback, her eyes glued to the page, oblivious to the rattling and shaking of the subway car. I peer at her, inspecting her features. I blink.

It can't be…

The hair is lighter, a warm brown and the blonde highlights are gone. Her auburn bangs sweep across her face. A beautifully decorated scarf of blue, gold and white hugs her neck and tucks into her unzipped army green parka. I search the girl's face for a Monroe piercing above the upper lip.

Check.

Soft, pouting lips.

Check.

Dark, animated eyes.

Check.

Holy shit.

My chest constricts. I breathe in deeply. I stare at Evelyn once. Twice. Three times. I press my Puma sneakers onto the subway floor. I envision myself slyly sliding off the seat and jumping off at the next station. I glance at Dave. He rummages through his knapsack.

Evelyn reads her book.

Fuck! What do I do?

I take another gander. She still hasn't spotted me. Dave digs deeper into his knapsack.

I have to say hi. It wouldn't be right not to.

I lean forward, tap her thigh and sit back down. Evelyn looks up. Her eyes bulge. She shakes her head as if waking up from a dream. My chest pounds.

"Hi!" Evelyn yelps. She drops her book onto the floor. I lean forward to grab it. She gets to it first.

"Hey." I smile.

Evelyn's voice shakes. "How are you? What are you doing here?"

"Doctor's appointment." I motion behind me as if Dr. Robertson's office is right there.

"Down here?"

My voice trembles. "Yup. What about you? Where you headed?"

Evelyn closes the book and places it on her lap. "Oh, I'm just coming back from Mississauga. I was working."

"Oh, that's weird." My voice shoots up an octave. "I'm heading back to sauga' actually." I feign a cough to clear my throat. The subway car rumbles, shooting through a tunnel. Bright, yellow lights flicker above our heads.

Evelyn raises her eyebrows. She eyes me, pursing her lips. "But... isn't Mississauga that way?" Evelyn points West. We're travelling Eastbound on the Bloor-Danforth line.

"Um." I look towards the entrance Dave and I got on at. "No?" My throat closes. "Oh, right." I laugh. "I'm going to St. George though. Gonna' take the shuttle back."

"Wouldn't you take the GO Train though?"

"Um, no." I rub my sweaty palms on my jeans. "The shuttle is free so I take that. GO Train is expensive."

Evelyn nods and stuffs the novel into her purse. "Right, it's like what six, seven bucks?"

"Yeah, and TTC fare is only three."

"Right, I see. Cool."

"Yeah."

The train jolts us as it whips around a sharp turn. Evelyn casts a glance at Dave out of the corner of her eye. Black headphones plug his ears as he flips through The Metro newspaper, leaving us to chat.

Neither of us bothers to fill in the gap of the last four months of our lives. Neither of us acknowledges the Facebook message Evelyn sent me telling me that what we had was fun, a lesson worth learning, how she thanked me and told me that I was 'cool'. That I contacted Alex to try and beg her for forgiveness, but never heard back. How I was a wreck last semester and that it took me three months to let go of five weeks. How I hated her, missed her, dreamt of her and finally, let go of her.

We chat about future aspirations and our plans after graduation. The trembling in my body eases. Evelyn's voice climbs when she talks about studying at the New York School of Design after finishing her undergraduate degree in English and Anthropology at U of T. She smiles to herself when I tell her about the book that I'm writing.

"So you know Claire?" Evelyn blurts after a moment of silence.

I laugh. "Uh, yeah. Yeah, I do. Why? Did she bring it up or something?"

"Yeah, she was telling me how she met you at some New Year's Eve party. She was like yeah, I know Mary!"

"Yeah, she kept going on about this girl, Evelyn, she knew back from high-school and I was like, "What's her last name?" and she said Mackenzie and I was like 'Oh, yeah. I know her.'"

We chuckle and smile, our tight lips trying too hard.

"Yeah." Evelyn continues. "We bumped into each other in the village and it was one of those moments like 'Oh, you are? So am I!'"

"Very cool."

Neither of us is aware that we are on the verge of dating the same girl, the same friend of Claire's who I hooked up with on New Year's Eve, the same lesbian who asked Evelyn out a few weeks ago. But, that's another story.

The train screeches to a halt.

"St. George Station," the intercom announces.

"Oh, right." I stand up and signal Dave to get up. "Are you getting off here?"

Evelyn slings her bag over her shoulder and stands up. "Yeah."

I blink.

Damn. She's short.

Evelyn leads the way out of the train. Passengers swarm in and out of the doorway. Evelyn and I walk side by side across the cement platform with Dave close behind. We approach the set of stairs to switch lines. I shake my head. "It's so weird bumping into you!"

Evelyn frowns. "I'm sorry." Her voice waivers.

"What?" I stare down at her. "What for?"

Evelyn shrugs, her eyes downcast. "For bumping into you."

"No. Don't be silly. Why would you be sorry?"

"I dunno..." Evelyn's voice trails off.

I follow her up the crowded staircase to the Yonge-University-Spadina line. I grab hold of the railing and spot Evelyn's brown leather purse. She bought it at the leather market in Florence on the second last day of our trip. A blue and yellow satin Tartuca flag wraps around the straps. I smile and tug on the soft, shiny material.

"Nice flag." I raise my voice, but a roar of voices fills the tunnel. Evelyn climbs the staircase. We stop at the second level.

"I'm going this way." Evelyn tilts her head.

"Okay."

Crowds of people pour out of the train doors and shove their way past us. Evelyn turns left and pushes her way through the crowd. I take a step forward.

Does she want me to follow her?

Evelyn twists and turns, dodging strangers as she strides ahead.

I stop, and I watch the girl with soft brown hair in an unzipped, army green parka disappear into the crowd. I spin around. Dave waits.

"Well, that was Evelyn. Live in the flesh." I clutch my backpack straps with trembling arms.

"That's the girl?!" Dave pokes his head past a pillar to get a better look at her. "Damn, Mary. She's pretty cute."

"Yeah." My eyes widen. "I know."

A man in his late twenties mutters at us under his breath. I slide out of the way. He walks around me and rushes down the steps. A group of students in grey dress pants and white dress shirts run past us and hop onto the train. I scan the cement pillars for a TTC map or sign indicating the direction of the train. I run my fingers along the yellow line and stop at Queen's Park. I turn around. The doors seal shut and the train screeches past us.

"Fuck," I mutter. "That was our train. Sorry."

"Way to be on the ball, Mary." Dave grins. "She's standing right over there you know." Dave points to the opposite side of the platform.

"Really?" I turn and spot her standing alone, texting on her cell phone. "Well fuck, I don't know if she wanted me to say bye or not. I'm not going over there now."

Dave shrugs. "Alright."

The next train pulls in.

"You alright, Mary? You seem a bit off."

We take a seat at the nearest bench. The train is packed with rush-hour commuters. "It just threw me a bit. I can't believe I just saw her." I shake my head. "So weird."

"Yeah, well that's life."

Dave brings up writing, publications, our books, graduation and how hard it's going to be to land a good job in our field. I drift in and out of focus. Italy is on my mind again.

***

Dave and I walk along St. George Street. Across the road, salted pathways snake through the snow covered grass in Queens Park. The homeless sleep on wet benches and students with backpacks stroll past us. Tall skyscrapers loom over us and an ambulance siren whizzes past our ears. My LG Rumour cell phone vibrates from inside my jacket pocket.

Text Message Received

Fr: Evelyn

Thought you'd be behind me when I turned around but you weren't so… Bye! *hug* it was nice to see you! You look well.

I groan.

Figures.

Dave walks beside me with his hands tucked into his jacket pockets. "Oh." Dave chuckles. "Well look at that. You gonna' text her back?"

"Obviously." I shoot him a dirty look. "I'm not gonna' be a douche."

"Hey, hey." Dave raises his arms. "Don't take it out on me now. Jesus."

I dodge puddles and re-type the message four times, adding a word here, removing a friendly intonation there. I shut my eyes and tap the send button.

Text Message Sent

Fr: Mary

Sorry. You disappeared on me. I was trying to catch the train. Nice seeing you too.

The sidewalk veers right. Dave and I trudge across the soggy grass and hop down the stone staircase leading to Hart House. We wait for the next shuttle bus to take us home. My LG Rumour vibrates in my hand, sings a jingle and the Bell Mobility Logo glows. The screen shuts off. I shake my head and smile.

Battery dead.

About the Author

Mary Dytyniak lives in Toronto, Ontario, Canada with her partner Diana and their dog Riley. She works in Marketing & Communications at York University and hopes to be a full-time author one day. She still loves to travel and and is always open to new experiences, wherever they may take her.